Framing The Struggle

Framing The Struggle

✦

Essays on the Middle East and the US media

Ahmed Bouzid

iUniverse, Inc.
New York Lincoln Shanghai

Framing The Struggle
Essays on the Middle East and the US media

iUniverse, Inc.

For information address:
iUniverse, Inc.
2021 Pine Lake Road, Suite 100
Lincoln, NE 68512
www.iuniverse.com

ISBN: 0-595-27215-0

Printed in the United States of America

For my family, here and in Algeria

Contents

Acknowledgements

Many thanks go to a long list of people who have tirelessly and selflessly worked to promote the Palestinian cause and to help Palestine Media Watch push forward with its mission of fighting for better media coverage of the conflict.

First, my thanks go to the PMWatch group leaders: Hatem Abunimeh, Baha Abushaqra, Tanweer Akram, Rima Anabtawi, Rania Awwad, Rasha Ayouby, Jonathan Bagot, Shari Barghouty, Brian Bogart, Michael Brown, Mohamed Bugaighis, Rani El-Hajjar, Ahmed El-Shimi, Majid Faraj, Vanessa Floyd, Edith Garwood, Adil Hajjoubi, Charlee Hathaway-Bevington, Tanya C. Hsu, Rizk Ikhrais, Mats Johansson, Fadi Kiblawi, Saira Kingston, Ibrahim Koshy, Mary Kraus, Standish Lawder, Sherri Muzher, David Nassar, Thomas Olson, Joseph Policano, Lane Pope, Seth Price, Issam Shahrouri, Raja Swamy, Bruce Weaver, Samantha Williams, and Dan Wolf.

I also want to thank the following people for their help and guidance: Susan Abulhawa, Ahmed Amr, Lamis Andoni, Omar Barghouti, Ramzy Baroud, Marda Dunsky, Tait Graves, Samir Moukaddam, Ray Hanania, Ali Khan, Jeff Mendez, Mark Miller, Mazin Qumsiyeh, Mouin Rabbani, and Cy and Lois Swartz.

Special thanks go to the PMWatch Advisory Board: Dr. Hanan Ashrawi, Dr. Salman Abu Sitta, Dr. Mustafa Barghouti, Prof. Noam Chomsky, Prof. Norman G. Finkelstein, Prof. Edward S. Herman, and Prof. Tanya Reinhart

And last but not least, my thanks go to the hundreds of media gadflies who day in and day out, with their letters and phone calls, struggle quietly but with impressive determination, for better media coverage of the conflict.

The right of return: Israel and Palestine

"What is vital for us," said an Israeli cabinet minister recently, "is to obtain the most important thing, the renunciation by the Palestinians of the right of return of refugees to territory under Israeli sovereignty…This right of return is our greatest concern because we want to maintain the character and the Jewish majority in Israel and renouncing this right is the only way to achieve that."

The quote would be upsetting enough if it had come from the hawkish Benjamin Netnayahu or the ultra-hawkish Ariel Sharon. In fact, the quote comes from Yuli Tamir, an Israeli cabinet minister close to Ehud Barak and one of the stars of the so-called left-wing peace camp. Moreover, had the speaker been from any country other than Israel (or the United States), and had the target population been any other than the Palestinians, the US media would probably be up in arms denouncing the statement as a shockingly racist and brazen example of state-sponsored ethnic cleansing. "How can such talk be heard even now, after all the painful lessons of this century!" would be the collective exclamation (as it was when the Milosevic regime was uttering similar pronunciations during the Bosnian war). But since the cabinet minister pronouncing those words is from Israel—and the Israeli Left at that!—the remarks go unnoticed, not surprisingly.

It is important to remember in all of this a basic reality: Israel explicitly subordinates citizenship to race. According to the Law of Return of the State of Israel, all Jews as well as spouses and children of Jews are entitled to what is called *Aliyah*—return to Israel. A Jewish person—any Jewish person—from anywhere around the world, can immigrate to Israel and practically obtain automatic Israeli citizenship with little difficulty. It does not matter if the immigrant had never set foot on Israeli soil, or even if any of his or her ancestors going back hundreds of years had never been to Israel either; by mere virtue of *being* Jewish, the person is entitled to live in "the land of Israel". Israel, moreover, is the only country in the world today that has adopted, as a matter of official policy, the pursuit of a certain racial makeup of its citizenry: i.e., maintaining a Jewish majority.

This policy, as is well known outside of the United States, is of course in direct violation of The International Convention on Elimination of All Forms of Racial Discrimination, which explicitly prohibits "any distinction, exclusion, restriction or preference based on race, color, descent, or national or ethnic origin." But Minister Tamir's statement violates another set of basic principles of International Law, articulated in The Universal Declaration of Human Rights. Here are a couple. Article 13, for instance, holds that: (1) "Everyone has the right to freedom of movement and residence within the borders of each state;" and (2) "Everyone has the right to leave any country, including his own, and to return to his country." Minister Tamir wishes to deny Palestinians their right to return to the homes from which they were forced to flee. Article 17 holds that: (1) "Everyone has the right to own property alone as well as in association with others;" and (2) "No one shall be arbitrarily deprived of his property." Minister Tamir wishes to deprive Palestinians of lands and houses for which they still hold, to this day, legal deeds.

Irony of ironies, Yuli Tamir is in fact Israeli's Minister of immigrant absorption: that is, she is in charge of overseeing the implementation and management of Israel's Law of Return. And yet, she denies Palestinians with valid property deeds to land and houses their most fundamental right of reclaiming what is rightfully theirs.

Perhaps now, more than ever before, Israelis should ponder the words uttered by the father of their nation, David Ben-Gurion. Just before he died, Ben-Gurion said: "[Israel] is two things. An ark and a Covenant…There are some who see Israel's importance primarily as an Ark, a place where the persecuted can go…I think the covenant takes precedence over the concept of refuge…Israel cannot just be a refuge. If it is to survive as a valid nation, it has to be much, much more…"

—December 25, 2002 (MediaMonitors.net)

The American people vs. the spinmeisters

Polls conducted in July and December, 2000, by Zogby International, found the following: to the question, "Do you agree or disagree that Palestinians have this right to return?", a whopping 74% of participants answered with either strongly agree" (52.1%) or "somewhat agree" (21.9%). That is, 3 out of 4 Americans believe that the Palestinians do have a right to return to their land, and more than one out of two Americans strongly hold that belief.

Treading away from the real world and into the never-never land of the editorial and opinion pages of America's most prestigious newspapers, we discover an altogether different perspective on the Palestinians' right of return.

The New York Times, for example, in its December 27, 2000 editorial, called the idea of Palestinians returning to their home "unrealistic". "A better approach," the Times wrote, "would be to put together an international compensation and resettlement package for these refugees, housing as many of them as practical within the borders of the new Palestinian state." The Times moreover did not flinch from explaining to us why it felt that a Palestinian return was "unrealistic": it "would threaten Israel's character as a Jewish state," the editorial explained, as though there were nothing remarkable about a modern state, and a democracy at that, explicitly pursuing a policy of maintaining a religiously-based "national character"!

The Washington Post, on its part, as always eager to remain competitively on-par with the New York Times in the sport of pro-Israel pamphleteering, has hailed Barak's latest maneuvers as "a remarkable compromise" (Dec. 31, 2000). The Post does not bother to enlighten us on exactly what Barak has compromised on, given that the Prime Minister has not tired of repeating the refrain that he will never cede sovereignty of the Temple Mount, nor will he ever let Palestinian refugees return to their land. All the same, the Post pushes on. In a startling wholesale adoption of Israel's long standing policy of creating facts of the ground, the

Post writes, and without a hint of embarrassment, that "the more Jewish settlements in the occupied territories grow, the less flexible Israel will be with land," as though settlements pop up and grow like mushrooms, just like that, all by themselves, rather than with the careful subsidy, supervision and encouragement of the Israeli government. Room for more Jewish settlements does exist, the Post believes, but "millions of Palestinian refugees cannot possibly be accommodated in Israel."

Amos Perlmutter, one of the most ardent mouthpieces of the Israeli Right in the United States, wrote in his December 27, 2000, column in the Washington Times that a Palestinian return to Israeli land "will change the demographic balance of power in Israel and will bring an end to Jewish statehood and to Zionism." Mincing his words not one bit, Mr. Perlmutter wrote: "Zionism was a philosophy of Jewish empowerment. The founding fathers of Israel and their successors up to Mr. Barak were dedicated to preserving the essence of a Jewish state, which means a Jewish majority in Israel." A true enough description of Zionism, but certainly no explanation why the whole world should subscribe to the Zionist ideal. Milosevic tried to argue once, along remarkably similar lines, for the need to maintain his nation's Serbian character, and we all know what that brought him: ridicule, a warrant for his arrest from the Hague, and the eventual collapse of his criminal regime.

Putting the matter in equally inflammatory terms, Yossi Klein Halevi of the New Republic wrote in The Los Angeles Times (Jan. 4th) that "the right of return is a euphemism for the destruction of Israel through demographic assault." George Will, another irredentist scribe well known for his unyielding pro-Israeli stands, managed to outdo even himself, when he wrote in the January 2 issue of Newsweek that "acknowledging a 'right of return' would be, for Israel, demographic suicide." In fact, damning the torpedoes, George Will went ahead and took out the precious (and yet often used) Holocaust card, by concluding his essay with: "Pessimists are realists who worry that, for the portion of world Jewry gathered in Israel, history may have saved its worst for last."

And even Richard Cohen, usually a vigorous voice against any form of racism or discrimination, simply threw up his hands—and his principles—in his column of January 4, where he wrote: "Israel cannot remain a Jewish state if about 4 million Palestinians are given the right to live there."

The American people have always stood in sympathy with Israel. In the Zogby poll mentioned above, those who identified themselves as sympathetic with the Israelis outnumbered those who said they were sympathetic with the Palestinians by a margin of 3 to 1. And yet, in spite of their bias in favor of Israel, average Americans have been consistently able to overcome that bias and have courageously stood on principle by agreeing that Palestinians indeed do have a right to return. If only America's opinion spinners could display such moral courage and such humane wisdom!

—January 8, 2001 (MediaMonitors.net)

No Honeymoon for George W.
Bush in the Middle East

By far the most important problem George W. Bush will initially face as president of the United States is the crisis in Middle East. A stable Middle East is one of the basic linchpins of a stable US economy, and in these nervous times of sagging consumer confidence and slowing growth, the last thing Mr. Bush needs is a stock market nervous about the world's energy supply.

Indeed, the two longest recessions America endured since 1929 were the 16 month contractions from November 1973 to March 1975 and from July 1981 to November 1982. Both were largely ignited by an oil crisis on the world market. Back in 1990, George Bush Senior had this well in mind when he mobilized the US armada to protect American oil interests in the Gulf region. Once president, George W. Bush faces a much more intractable problem that no smart bomb can take out: the Palestinian-Israeli conflict.

If matters follow their expected course, Ariel Sharon will be elected Prime Minister of Israel barely two weeks after George W. Bush is sworn in. Mr. Sharon's accession to the leadership of the Israeli government will mark not only the final collapse of the Oslo peace process, but the undoing of the first Camp David accords, signed back in September 1978, between Anwar Sadat and Manachem Begin. Ariel Sharon is held directly responsible throughout the Arab and Muslim worlds for the massacre of hundreds of Palestinian civilians in Sabra and Shatilla during Israel's 1982 Lebanon invasion. He elicits from Palestinians, Arabs, and Muslims in general deep, visceral loathing comparable in intensity to the loathing Jews have for Hitler. With Sharon at the helm of the Israeli government, no Palestinian, Arab or Muslim leader would dare engage his government in any official talks or negotiations, public or otherwise. And the last person who would entertain being seen in Mr. Sharon's company, let alone be seen shaking hands with him, is Yasir Arafat.

With no prospects for a peaceful resolution, the Palestinian Intifada will have no choice but to press on, its passions and energies further fueled by the ominously promised harsh crackdown from the unyielding Sharon. The escalation in violence will then put enormous pressure on all Arab countries, from Morocco to Jordan, to Syria, Iraq, Lebanon, Yemen, and Saudi Arabia, along with non-Arab Muslim countries such as Pakistan, Iran, Afghanistan, and Malaysia, to react with something more than mere words. Arab public opinion is already distraught over their leadership's inaction during this three-month old uprising. With Ariel Sharon—in their eyes the "Butcher of Sabra and Shatilla"—ordering and supervising the crackdown on the Intifada, Arab and Muslim public opinion will no longer be content with fiery speeches of solidarity with Palestinians: they will want action.

Chances are that an all out crack down on Palestinians from a Sharon government would first result in the collapse of the remaining diplomatic relations that have been established and nurtured between Israel and some Arab states for the past decade—and in the case of Egypt, for the last two decades. Morocco has drastically reduced its contact with Israel since the outbreak of the uprising, and would be the first to completely sever them at all levels. Jordan would probably be the next to follow, reluctant as King Abdallah may be to take that step, while Egypt's Mubarak—forever battling his 'fundamentalist demons'—would have no choice but to fold his Tel Aviv tent, bite the bullet, and give up the two billion American dollars for the sake of his political survival.

Beyond that point, a further continued assault on the Palestinians—especially now that the Arab masses have joined the satellite-knit globe and are intimately in the know about what is taking place to the Palestinians on an hourly basis—will place huge pressures on the Arab leadership to act with more than toothless diplomatic measures. And their leadership will have no choice but to act: either by militarily mobilizing against Israel or by cracking down on the popular challenge that would undoubtedly surge if they decide not to mobilize.

Either way, George W. Bush is in for the most unstable Middle East since the break out of war in 1973.

—January 23, 2001

Elie Wiesel: no lover of humanity

I remember a few years ago, in the dark of the Bosnian genocide night, Charlie Rose asked Elie Wiesel in a one-on-one interview with him whether he felt that the genocidal mass killing of Bosnians could be equated with the Holocaust. The question itself is one of those absurdities that only people who make their living asking questions would pose with a straight face, but Elie Wiesel did not think it was silly or absurd. He paused dramatically, as he only knows how, lowered his eyes and reflected, and then, with a wounded, pained grimace, and of course with great sadness, responded that, no, one cannot compare the two. The Holocaust was something beyond anything. It was not that the lives of the Holocaust victims were more precious than those of Bosnians, but rather that the Holocaust was something special in history, that it stood by itself, above all other man-made human catastrophes.

I remember shaking my head in shock and disbelief at what I was hearing. The question may have been absurd, but the answer was clearly wrong and immoral, especially coming from a man who has made a living and a career at being the world's Czar on morality and human suffering. There was one, and only one correct and moral answer to that absurd question: all killings of the innocent are Holocausts, no matter how small, no matter who the victims are, no matter their age, or of what race or gender they may be—killing the innocent is a sin, and will always be a sin. Instead, Elie Wiesel preferred to defend his turf, to reduce the Holocaust to a historical event rather than elevate it to a symbol for all humanity—i.e., he preferred to jealously guard what he felt was his own.

Up until his January 24, 2001, column in the New York Times, "Jerusalem in my heart", Elie Wiesel by and large remained silent on the crisis in the Occupied Territories and Israel. Indeed, he himself notes in his column that this behavior has earned him many a scolding "for not protesting whenever Israeli police or soldiers react excessively to violence from Palestinian soldiers or civilians." But, the quiescent Wiesel tells us, "My critics have their conception of social and individual ethics; I have mine." The rest of his article tells us exactly the sort of ethics that animate Mr. Wiesel's conscience: the very same ethics that led him to subli-mate the Jewish Holocaust above all other sufferings, and to subordinate the genocide of Bosnians to a lower category of human pain.

On Jerusalem and the Palestinians' right of return, Nobel Peace Prize winner Elie Wiesel and war-monger/abettor of massacres, Ariel Sharon, differ not one whit. Jerusalem is not that important to Muslims, he says, adopting the most vulgar arguments from the most vulgar pro-Sharon right-wingers. Arabs are only now mentioning Jerusalem, when they have always neglected it, he says, mimicking the hysterical ranting of one-trick scribes that never tire of repeating the same drivel. He rehashes a convenient history, in which Israel offered its hand in peace only to be rebuffed by Arabs thirsty for Jewish blood, and in which 600,000 Pal-estinians left of their own accord rather than flee in fear and panic the murderous onslaught of Israeli soldiers and Jewish settlers. As for the Palestinians' right of return, Mr. Wiesel has no qualms saying what's on his mind: "To many Israelis, that would be tantamount to suicide."

And so religion—Jerusalem's place in Judaism—trumps not only international law (which has always considered all of Jerusalem Occupied Territory) but the most basic right for self-determination of those who inhabit the city, those who have seen their land confiscated, their houses taken over by newly arriving Jews, or demolished. And so also race—the need to maintain the Jewish character of Israel—trumps international law and the most basic of human rights. Jews from anywhere in the world have a right to "return" to an Israel they have never set foot upon, while those Palestinians with deeds in hand, deep historical roots, and living ties to their land and property will need to accept their fate and go some-where else.

What can one say but this: Shame on Mr. Wiesel, the Holocaust survivor, who suffered under the hands of those who asserted glory and pride above humanity, but who now forgets.

Shame on Wiesel, the Holocaust survivor, who suffered under the hands of those who denied his humanity and who drove him from his land and his home, but who now forgets.

Shame on him a thousand times for mimicking his old-executioners. He has no love but for his own kind—a man who puts dusty glories above simple human-ity—a man who stays silent as children's skulls are crushed and their bones shattered by bullets, but who all of a sudden speaks with a shrill voice because he feels his cherished memories threatened.

Mr. Wiesel once said: "Sometimes we must interfere. When human lives are endangered, when human dignity is in jeopardy, national borders and sensitivities become irrelevant. Whenever men or women are persecuted because of their race, religion, or political views, that place must—at that moment—become the center of the universe."

It is clear now more than ever that Mr. Wiesel was not speaking for or about all of humanity. He was speaking for his own kind, his own people—only!

Mr. Wiesel: surrender at once your badge as spokesman for humanity's conscience.

—January 26, 2001

On irony and the bulldozer of history: a letter to Ariel Sharon

Dear Mr. Sharon:

The irony is thick, everyone laments now, with you at the head of the government: how ironic that your very reckless act of September 28th, they say, has propelled you to the very pinnacle of power—and more importantly for you, of prestige and respect! How ironic, they say, that your very brutality, your very racist bigotry, your contempt for Palestinian life and welfare, your expansionist drive, your qualities as a man of violence and not as a man of peace, have attracted an angry electorate to your message of "peace through strength". How ironic. Of course, Yassir Arafat and the Palestinians are the ones to blame, as always: they should have known better than to spurn the generous Barak, we are told. They saw you coming all along and yet they didn't blink, and so now they have you to contend with. Irony of ironies, they say, how in their fight to liberate themselves, the Palestinians have brought to power the one man who will not and cannot listen to their cries for freedom. And now, they reap what they have sown.

And yet, we all know that the wheels of history do not stop with an election, nor are they jammed by a thick irony. You know that full well, Arik, as you sit on top the world today, when once you wallowed in the mire of ignominy. After all, what is history if not a heap of ironies piled one on top of the other?

And so, once your absurd tenure has expired its last vile breath, history will note a thicker irony still: how your final demise was brought about by your very ascension to the premiership. Where once only Palestinians and Arabs knew of your crimes against humanity, now the whole world will know them in their full glorious gore. Now that you are no longer merely an eccentric bully but a prime minister, career hungry reporters and young scholars will dig into your past and resurrect those ghosts that have much to tell. Ask Pinochet: he thought the world had forgotten after twenty seven years—but it hadn't. Now, he fakes dementia and clings to his few fascist supporters for a scrap of dignity. But he knows he will go down in history as a villain, not a hero. And so will you.

History will also note another irony: just as Ehud Barak's crackdown on the Intifada guaranteed that the Intifada will intensify, so your election to the premiership will only strengthen Palestinian resolve to push on with the resistance. And you, of all people, should know better: you have driven them out of their homes, confiscated their land and demolished their houses, forced them into exile, killed and maimed them, perpetrated massacres against them, poisoned their life and strangled their freedom with settlements deep inside their land—and yet, they have not relented and they have not submitted! And so, instead of stemming the tide, history will duly note that your arrival ushered an era of unprecedented solidarity, not only among Palestinians, but among all Arabs and Muslims.

Yet another irony that history will surely not fail to note will be the disgrace that your election brought upon the Israeli people as a whole. You won by a 20% landslide—a record. And it is clear why you won. You won because you convinced the electorate that you are ready to mete out more punishment to the indigenes who stubbornly refuse to accept their assigned lot. And so, where once Israel was viewed as a bulwark of civilization and democracy in a sea of third world tribalism, now the truth comes out that deep down Israel is nothing of the sort but a mere colonial outpost, functioning very much along the classic lines of a racist imperial presence.

And perhaps irony of ironies, and the biggest blow of all, will turn out to be that your election will make the task of whitewashing Israel and absolving it of all misdeeds, big and small, that much more intractable. Your dear friends in the United States have been clamoring for you to head Israel since time immemorial. Well, their wish has now come true. But now they may very well be wondering if it was a wise wish to have in the first place, when all is said and done. How can one defend a war criminal? How can one defend a killer of civilians? Ehud Barak is gone—the so-called "dove"—and with him are gone the last few remaining thin curtains behind which Israel's defenders have been hiding. You promised to make but the most meager and miserly of offers, so no more bashing Arafat for spurning generosity. Your have made it clear that you will not refrain from using force, so no more claims of restraint. Irony of ironies, with your election, you have taken from your friends all of their favorite weapons. And so, they stand now, unarmed, scratching their heads: how on earth to proceed.

Your tenure will be brief, Arik, and when you exit, you will discover that thanks to you, your fascist dreams of a Greater Israel and an extinguished Palestinian identity will have vanished with you forever into the dark of oblivion. History will go on, once you are out of the way, and history will record, as it has never failed to record, that a people fighting for their freedom and dignity always prevail, sooner or later.

History is the bulldozer, Arik, not you.

—February 9, 2001

Columbia, Nicaragua and Israel: parallels and lessons

Andres Oppenheimer, a Latin America correspondent for the Miami Herald, wrote recently in a column published by the Philadelphia Inquirer (Feb. 9, 2001) that "[at] least 3,000 people were killed in political violence [in Columbia] last year, and an additional 2,500 were kidnapped, many of them by [the Marxist guerilla group] FARC." Anyone who relies on the American press and its columnists for information about Columbia would find nothing notable in Mr. Oppenheimer's statement. Anyone who has access to other sources of information would immediately note that Mr. Oppenheimer's statement is so misleading that it borders on being a flat falsehood. Indeed, a detailed report issued by Human Rights Watch last year offers "detailed, abundant, and compelling evidence of continuing close ties between the Colombian Army and paramilitary groups responsible for gross human rights violations." A report issued by Amnesty International this past January states, "Paramilitary activity increased in 2000 and paramilitary groups were considered responsible for ninety-three massacres in the first five months of the year."

The distortions offered us by Mr. Oppenheimer are nothing new: back in the days of the Nicaragua Contras, we were told that most of the atrocities were perpetrated by the Sandanistas. A decade after the end of the conflict there, we know that the truth is the opposite: most of the atrocities were committed by the US-backed Contras and their various criminal cohorts in an effort to terrorize the population into abandoning the rebellion.

The truth about Columbia is remarkably similar. The pro-establishment factions and their paramilitary units benefit from massive financial support from the United States—to the tune of $1.9 billion of US taxpayer money. Moreover, according to Marcos Romero, spokesman for Paz Columbia—a coalition of more than 100 non-governmental human rights and environmental groups—"80% of the US aid is for purchasing helicopters and weaponry.... Only 20% of the money is going toward social programs."

The truth about Plan Columbia—the US-backed effort to quell the insurgency—is that it is undemocratic. "Plan Columbia was drafted in the US Senate and implemented by President Andres Pastrana," says Episcopalian priest Monsenor Jime Prieto, "but the people of Columbia were never consulted or included in this important decision.... The Plan is undemocratic...it does not represent a social investment in peace, but a plan for escalating the war."

The truth about Columbia, explains Almando Belwena, president of the National Organization of Indigenous Columbians (ONIC), is that "the main motivation behind the war is territory.... For five centuries, we indigenous have maintained our sovereignty and the been anti-imperialist. [But] now the Plan Columbia is escalating the war to new levels."

Bulwena puts it bluntly: "The [government] knows that it cannot negotiate with the indigenous to gain access to the natural resources on our lands. So, it is waging a war that is intended to kill us or drive us off the territory."

The one thing on which I agree with Mr. Oppenheimer is the parallel he draws between Columbian president Andres Pastrana and former Israeli Prime Minister Ehud Barak. But while Mr. Oppenheimer wishes us to believe that Mr. Pastrana and Mr. Barak are men of peace, well intentioned but lacking in backbone, reality tells us that they are not. Both Pastrana and Barak have come to the conclusion that honest negotiations will not bring them what they want, and so they have waged a war against indigenous peoples who will not submit. The Columbian resistance is demonized as "Marxist guerillas", the Palestinian resistance as "terrorist groups".

Mr. Oppenheimer fears the replication in Columbia of the Israeli swing to the right. But by calling on Mr. Pastrana to "[show] some back-bone and [begin] seriously cracking down on leftist and rightist guerillas," he is doing nothing less than pointing the way to the further escalation of bloodshed, with no prospect for anything resembling a lasting peace. Shimon Peres cracked down harshly on the Lebanese in operation Grapes of Wrath in Southern Lebanon, back in April 1996, just before the May elections that year, desperately trying to demonstrate that he was not soft; alas that did nothing but escalate the violence. As a result, he was roundly defeated by Benjamin Netanyahu. Ehud Barak tried the same strategy for the past four months against the Palestinians. The result was a massive landslide defeat delivered to him by someone most Israelis considered just a few months ago the least plausible candidate to the premiership. The swing to the far right in Israel is indeed no fiction, but the cause is clear: the notion that problems can be forced into a solution if only more force were applied against an indigenous population that understands force, and only force.

The Columbians have endured 36 years of conflict; the Palestinians 52. It is time that something new was tried both in Columbia and in the Middle East. One suggestion: start listening to the indigenous populations and abandon the notion that force is the only thing they understand.

—February 12, 2001

Colin Powell: a shift in US Mideast policy?

The very first question posed to Colin Powell after George W. Bush announced him as his nominee for the post of Secretary of State concerned the Middle East. In answering it, Colin Powell seemed to be delivering the usual pre-packaged, sanitized response, but if one listened carefully, one could detect an undertone that at least slightly differed from the one that Albright, Clinton, or Gore had been using with remarkable consistency for the past eight years. Any of those three would have answered it by saying, first, that all violence must cease, second, that both sides must return to the negotiating table, and third, that the United States remains firmly committed first and foremost to Israel's security. Colin Powell's answer shifted things around slightly, but not insignificantly: first, he stated the obligatory "the United States is a good friend of Israel", delivering it in a surprisingly perfunctory tone, but then he added : "but the Palestinians also have concerns that need to be listened to and addressed." Unremarkable as his statement may sound, anyone who had been following the language, emphases and vocabulary the Clinton administration had been using when talking about the Israeli/Palestinian conflict would not have failed to pick up the subtle nuance.

Since then, Colin Powell has clearly been sending messages that things are not as they used to be. Indeed, only a few hours after seven Israeli soldiers and an Israeli civilian were killed on February 14 by a Palestinian bus driver, Colin Powell reiterated that the most important step towards bringing the vicious cycle of bloodshed and violence to an end is to address the severe economic hardship that Palestinians have been enduring for decades. Had Albright, Clinton, or Gore been at the microphone, we would no doubt have instead heard the usual tiresome screed about the evils of terrorism, the need to ensure the security of Israel, and an urgent call for Arafat to bring the bloodshed to an end. That an American Secretary of State would spend the better part of his answer to a question regarding the killing of eight Israelis by talking about Palestinian suffering is something to take note of, to say the least.

Does this mean that we are witnessing a shift in America's position? Not necessarily. Shifts in policy do not occur overnight. But what is certain is that all the main elements are now present for a potential important change in American policy regarding the Middle East conflict.

First, the election of Ariel Sharon to the premiership has done away with the false premise that Israel is committed to a peace process that will quickly bring finality to the conflict and relief for the Palestinians. What Ariel Sharon means when he says he is willing to engage the Palestinians in peace talks, is simply that he is willing to engage them in a series of interim agreements that will take years, if not decades, to implement. Of course, what Ariel Sharon is proposing is nothing more than a return to the status quo ante—i.e., to a policy of quiet creeping annexation of Palestinian lands, of confiscation of Palestinian property—and most importantly, of building settlements, and more settlements. That is why the ending of violence is an essential pre-requisite to any peace talks as far as Mr. Sharon and his government are concerned: as long as there is violence in the colonies, the eyes of the world will remain on Israel's behavior and actions. And that is precisely why the Palestinians have refused to abandon their struggle.

Second, the economy is not ready for an oil crisis. Indeed, the two longest recessions America endured since 1929 were the 16 month contractions from November 1973 to March 1975 and from July 1981 to November 1982. Both were largely ignited by an oil crisis on the world market. Back in 1990, George Bush Senior mobilized the US armada to protect American oil interests in the Gulf region. Now, George W. Bush faces a much more intractable problem that no smart bomb can take out: the Palestinian-Israeli conflict. The necessity of heading off another oil crisis must be high on Colin Powell's agenda as he tackles the Middle East conflict in the months and years to come.

And third, and most importantly: this Intifada, make no mistake about it, is a war for independence. And like all true wars of independence, it is being waged by the people, with their leadership doing all they can to catch up with them, lest they lose control. Putting down a guerilla insurgency is tough enough. Putting down the uprising of a whole people is impossible.

Facing an inflexible Ariel Sharon, a shaky economy, and a Palestinian people determined to take matters into their own hands and push forward for their own independence, the current US administration confronts a beast altogether different from the one Bill Clinton and his team faced only a year ago. Back then, the so-called "dovish" Barak stood as the epitome of a seemingly benign Israel striving hard to achieve peace, the US economy roared, while the Palestinians as usual patiently and quietly waited for their leadership to deliver on their promises. That world is long gone now. What remains is naked, stark reality: a dispossessed people committed to struggling for their freedom and facing brutal occupation and deadly suppression.

Have George W. Bush and Colin Powell grasped this qualitative shift and will they act accordingly? Early indications are that they may have. But only the coming weeks and months will reveal more clearly if America will finally begin to nudge away from its usual mindless catering to Israeli ambitions and towards a policy based on rationality and long-term self-interest.

—February 16, 2001

Violence in words

Where should you go to read calls for outright ethnic cleansing and population transfer, blood libels, blatantly racist slurs, open agitation for regicide, and incitement to use deadly force against civilians? Belgrade's "Glas Novosti", Baghdad's "Al-Jumhuriyyah", Rwanda's "World Wide Gazeteer"? Try North America's most respected publications.

Ethnic cleansing: in a piece titled "A coalition of terror", published by the Washington Times on June 6, 2001, Cal Thomas wrote: "The Jews have misplaced their faith. Gifted with thinking the best about human potential, Jews have made decisions that too often are not in their interests—such as allowing mortal enemies to live among them and giving up land seized for their own protection after five wars and numerous terrorist attacks...Israel should declare its intention to transfer large numbers of its Palestinian residents to Arab nations." A perfectly rational argument very much on par with Milosevic's rationale for transferring his alleged "mortal enemies" from Bosnia, so that peace can at long last reign among an ethnically pure Serb population.

Blood libel: a May 23rd column by Jonathan Kellerman published in the Los Angels Times equated calls by the international community, human rights organizations, peace activists in Israel and beyond, to dismantle illegal settlements in Palestinian territory with Hitler's Judenrein policy: "Strip away the label 'settlers' and substitute 'Jews'" Mr. Kellerman wrote, "and the pronouncements of ostensibly right-thinking people degrade to: Peace will come to the region only if Jews are expelled from areas where their presence inflames Palestinians. In other words, ethnic cleansing." Imagine if Kellerman's argument had been used against those who called for Saddam Hussein's invading forces to be expelled from Kuwait. Even Baghdad's Al-Jumhuriyyah was not so imaginative!

Racism: Palestinians, Arabs, and Muslims have been routinely demonized and stereotyped in the North American press in shockingly raw terms and images that bring what we thought was the distant, unpleasant past of violent racism to the living present. As Toronto-based writer and broadcaster Michael Coren wrote back in October of last year: "The fact is that in North America and most of the Western world the Arab peoples are not treated at all fairly and seem to be the final example of where racism is permissible, even respectable." An understatement, to say the least, if one were to take a look at a cartoon published on June 5th by the Canadian Edmonton Journal. In it, Arabs and Palestinians were labeled as "Murderous", "Evil", "Assassins", "Killers", and "Animals". Replace the words "Arab" from that cartoon by any other ethnic label and chances are that the editorial board would never have allowed the cartoon to run. Why did it in this case: because the targets are mere Palestinians and Arabs, not worthy of the same decency extended to other ethnic groups.

Regicide: in his Washington Times June 7 piece, "Rationale for regicide?", Amos Perlmutter, professor of Political Science at the American University in Washington, informed us that "Mr. Arafat himself is the most impoverished little peanut, a ruthless one." Equating Hitler and Stalin with Arafat, thus trivializing the evil of two demons and demonizing the official and elected representative of a people without a land or an army, Mr. Perlmutter went on to argue: "Hitler fought the war to the last moment of his life, killing millions of Germans and allies. Stalin died trying to kill the Jews of Russia. Once they died, the bleeding stopped and the utopian dream disappeared. Mr. Arafat must go…. He must fall on his own sword." That international law clearly stands against the assassination of leaders is too fine a point for Prof. Perlmutter to bother with.

Violence against civilians: in his April 20, 2001, Washington Post column titled, "What Happened to The Powell Doctrine?", Charles Krauthammer argued that Colin Powell's strategy of using "overwhelming force" should be adopted wholesale by Israel in dealing with the Palestinian uprising. "First we're going to cut it off," Mr. Krauthammer fondly recalled Powell's words, "Then we're going to kill it." The "it" that Mr. Powell was referring to was of course the Iraqi Army. But for Mr. Krauthammer, the "it" in the case of the Palestinian-Israeli conflict should refer to the Palestinian Intifada and all those who have participated in the uprising against continued Israeli occupation, the overwhelming majority of whom are civilians. The killing of nearly 500 Palestinians, as far as Mr. Krauthammer is concerned, is a sign of great "restraint" from the Israeli armed forces. Only with greater violence—and killing on a much larger scale—will the uprising be brought to a halt. A similar argument was articulated in The New York Times by a man Tim Russert loves to call "America's dean of journalism", William Safire. Mr. Safire wrote the following in his June 4, 2001 column: "With doves turned to realists and pressure from Bibi Netanyahu to defend the nation, and with Israelis unwilling to further expose their children to lives of terror, Sharon will let Sharon be Sharon." And who is the real Sharon? The man responsible for more than 17,000 Lebanese civilian deaths during the Israeli invasion of Lebanon, a man found by an Israeli court to be "personally responsible" for the massacre of hundreds of defenseless Palestinian refugees. Imagine urging the world to clamor for Milosevic to let Milosevoc be Milosevic so that the Bosnian headache can be brought to a swift conclusion!

Calls of ethnic cleansing, blood libels, raw racism, open agitation for regicide, and incitement to inflict more death and destruction upon civilians: such violent speech is openly tolerated by respected North American publications. But violence only begets more violence. We have seen this truism cruelly illustrated day in and day out in the Palestinian-Israeli conflict. Israelis kill Palestinians, destroy their homes and confiscate their land, and Palestinians retaliate with rocks, mortar shells, and suicide bombers. The cycle will not be broken unless and until violence—both in deed and in word—is deemed beyond the pale of civilized behavior.

—June 8, 2001

After Sharon, a Phoenix Arises

When historians write the final draft on the short and bloody tenure of Israeli Prime Minister Ariel Sharon, they will undoubtedly point to June 18, 2001, as a watershed moment.

That was the day a group of Palestinians brought a lawsuit in a Belgian court against Sharon for war crimes and crimes against humanity for his involvement in the September 1982 Sabra and Shatila massacres.

History will show that public opinion against Sharon began to build soon after that fateful day, with the first signs that he and his coalition were in deep trouble showing when he took his early July trip to Europe. During that trip, he was greeted by throngs of demonstrators chanting "Sharon assassin" and "Sharon to The Hague," while behind closed doors, and later publicly, European leaders flatly rejected Israel's policies.

Historians also will note something even more important: that Israel's relationship with its long-time guardian and custodian, the U.S., began to show evidence of strain. Historians will retrace the early indications of the rift to Feb. 25, the day Colin Powell shocked the Sharon administration by using the word "siege" to describe the Israeli blockade of Palestinian cities and villages.

They will then point to March 19 as another crucial date, when Powell delivered a speech to the American Israeli Political Action Committee (AIPAC), where he uttered the following fateful words: "The U.S. continues to support a comprehensive peace to the Middle East, one based on U.N. Security Council Resolutions 242 and 338 and the formula of land for peace." Mention of 242 and 338, historians will remind us, was hardly ever made during the eight years of the Clinton administration.

From then on, historians will explain, things began to unravel: In early May the Bush administration publicly condemned Israel for crossing into Palestinian territory; later, it strongly objected to the use of F16 fighter jets; later still, it supported an international commission's call for a total freeze on settlement building; then in June, the U.S. stated that it no longer opposed, in principle, Arafat's long-standing demand for international observers on the ground to monitor the situation; and in late July, as Israel heedlessly intensified its assassination policy, U.S. official displeasure mounted to such a crescendo that words such as "excessive," "highly provocative" and even "reprehensible" were being used by the State Department to denounce Israeli actions.

On the domestic front, historians will remind us that Sharon had been elected on the promise that he was going to bring security to Israel, but that in reality he accomplished the opposite: Israelis felt much less secure under him than they did under Ehud Barak or Benjamin Netanyahu. Even more important, the economic slide under Sharon continued unabated: Tourism in Israel fell and housing construction experienced a noticeable slump while investors, jittery about the potential of war with Syria, Lebanon and Iraq, held their financing away from a market badly in need of input.

Historians will point to the election of Ariel Sharon as the beginning of the end for the settlement movement and the creeping presence into the occupied territories. They will note that while Barak was able to underhandedly push the policy forward with great success (with no opposition from the U.S. administration), Sharon crudely blew the lid off the whole enterprise when he blockaded whole cities, shelled civilian buildings, rolled his tanks into Palestinian territory and deployed F16s against Palestinian targets.

What historians will no doubt relish most is the political resurrection of the historically unelectable Shimon Peres. They will note how the Machiavellian Peres inserted himself in Sharon's government, how he took over the foreign ministership and how he stood by his prime minister early on, but eventually began to publicly disagree with Sharon on key points: settlement freeze, the assassination policy and the effort to unseat Arafat.

What will follow is not difficult to predict: Historians will note that soon after the beginning of Sharon's rapid decline, Shimon Peres decided to bolt from the sinking ship, bringing with his exit the collapse of the rickety coalition and the unity government.

Once his alliance with Sharon is broken, Peres will stand as the only viable alternative in the eyes of Israelis—the only man capable of carrying the momentous historical mission of making the necessary compromise and closing a deal with the Palestinians. Disillusioned in Sharon's "security through strength" solution, Israelis will at long last take their first step away from forcing a military settlement on a political conflict.

As for the Sharon tenure, historians will tell us that without the bloody Sharon months that brought the whole region to the brink of disaster, Israel would never had dared to turn its back, once and for all, against its old, destructive habit of conquer and wait.

—August 7, 2001 (The Los Angeles Times)

A black day in September

A few minutes before 9:00 am, Tuesday morning, September 11: I am hurrying out the door, picking up my lunch box (in which my wife had just slipped a special tea brew that is supposed to speed up my recovery from a lingering cold). Out, the temperature is perfect, no humidity: it's gonna be a great day, I think. As I am walking to my car, I hear one of the painters working on the house opposite shouting to one of his colleagues: "so now they are saying it's a terroristic attack?" "Terroristic?", I pause. And I immediately know that something is wrong, even seriously wrong. Otherwise, why would workmen be talking about "terrorism", and one of them even shaking his head over it? Americans, especially when they are going about their work, don't waste their time talking about "terroristic attacks". And it must have happened here the United States. And if they are saying it's "terroristic", then it must have been huge.

I hurry to my car and turn the engine on. NPR. A report on Bush's scheduled stump tour for his education proposal. Hmmm, I think, couldn't have been that much of a big deal, after all. I warm the car and pull back. "We will of course keep you updated on the latest about the collision in New York of two commuter planes." "Hmmm," I think, "collision of commuter planes," an image of two small planes colliding with each other flashed in my mind, "that's not a big deal…."

All the way to the office, I alternate between thinking about the computer bug awaiting me at the office (I am a software developer) and listening to a report on the upcoming wrangling on the budget. My initial gut feeling that something big took place is fading away. I was wrong, and I feel a bit relieved. Then I remember the bumper sticker I had just put in the night before: "Free Palestine!". White on red. I look in the rear-view mirror at the SUV hovering behind me: wonder if they noticed it, if they are angry or supportive, or if they even care…. Well, at least they get to see the words "Free Palestine!" and maybe it will get them to realize that Palestinians are not asking for the moon, but just what they are entitled to—their freedom….

Then, at the parking lot, the horror is announced, simply: "two jetliners slammed against the Twin Towers. The Towers are in flames." I am stunned: the planes must have been hijacked, I think. There must have been passengers. Strangely, no report of casualties, no flight numbers, no speculation about who did it or why. Just like Oklahoma City, six years ago: only the thinnest strands of information....

I start hurriedly for the office. We have cable in our conference rooms. People must be huddled there. But then I stop: "The bumper sticker!", I remember. "What if...", and turn back, bend down, and rip it off without hesitation. "No need to invite trouble," I think, ashamed at my cowardice. "Americans are tolerant and lovely, as long as nothing is rocking their boat." That was something I had come to fully understand back in Desert Storm, when I was a grad student. Oklahoma City re-taught me the lesson. So, no need to invite trouble....

At the office, an eerie silence. A colleague informs me that "they are all watching TV". I make my tea and take my medicine, and proceed to join my colleagues.

Peter Jennings' voice is blaring out of the room. A dozen or so of my colleagues are there, watching with wide open eyes, silently.

Then the image of the towers in flame. My heart sinks. "This is bigger than Kennedy", I realize immediately. Things will never be the same again.

Peter Jennings is angry: at whom? "Why didn't the so-called terrorism experts pick this up," he scolds one such expert. The expert simply stutters that this is obviously a major intelligence failure, almost apologizing. Grins and hisses from my colleagues, though not at the expert, but at Jennings: "give the guy a break," one of my colleagues says.

Then the Pentagon is hit. "What is this," another colleague shakes his head: "are we under attack or something?" Nervous laughter.

An hour of this, as we sat transfixed, absorbing, ever slowly, the image of America's symbols of financial and military power reduced to rubble. America is like any other country after all, of flesh and blood, and open to attack.

Jennings tells us that the Popular Front for the Liberation of Palestine has claimed responsibility. A colleague gives a chuckle, and pokes at me good-naturedly: "Where is Ahmed?", she laughs. I laugh, but I am nervous.

But what are they really thinking? Are they angry? Americans give a good talk about being tolerant, but they are rarely tested. And it's hard to overcome instinctive feelings of fear and hatred towards someone from a seemingly threatening tribe if you had never practiced to overcome your irrational impulses. Everything is a matter of practice and training, good intentions notwithstanding. Back in desert storm, the FBI gave visits to ordinary Muslim activists, students, and regular civilians simply because they had an

Arabic-sounding name. That was a war far off. This is here, with the country in the grip of panic. God help us.

"It's not a good time to be Arab and Muslim," I let out. Loud laughter. I feel better.

"Thank God it's not the 13th," I think to myself, "the day of the signing of the Oslo Accords. Or the 28th, the first anniversary of the second Intifada." Reports of jubilant celebration in the West Bank: that's going to hurt for a long time to come, I think to myself. And the Israelis are going to have a field day with this. Who's going to stop them now? Palestinians should be crying, but I do understand why they are celebrating, just like I understood why African Americans cheered when OJ was found not guilty: the Palestinians are not cheering the death of Americans—just as African Americans were not cheering the freedom of a killer—but rather the humbling of their arrogant, hypocritical, mighty tormentor. And nothing gladdens the heart of the downtrodden than the sight of a fallen Colossus.

By lunch time, we are back to our desks. Security here has informed us that all but the main doors will be closed off. Some scoff (but not many): there is nothing here anyone will want to blow up.

At our desks, hushed conversations. "What goes around comes around," one says. But most are simply confused and stunned by the mere possibility that this could take place.

"You can't go around arming these terrorists," one of them says, "and not expect that one they will come back and use them against you." We all nod our heads.

"But the irony," I venture, "is that no arms were used. No missile shield could have done much to stop any of this." Nods and silence.

Lights are blinking at my phone: my wife orders me to take off the bumper sticker. "I already took it off," I confess to her sheepishly (only last night did I lecture her that one must stand for his principles). She doesn't lecture me, but tells me that her family (from China) and mine (from Algeria) had called, breathlessly asking if everything was ok. Friends from Canada also called. My brother from France called, too. But my wife is herself worried about a close friend who works at the Trade Center. "Their phone is busy," she complains. I try to reassure her that the circuits are busy in that area, but I am worried too. "Her office is at the 19th floor, though" she almost pleads. "Maybe she had a chance to get out fast."

And a feeling of horror overwhelms me: what if MY WIFE were working there? How could I take the agony of waiting for a phone call, and not knowing what happened while watching the collapse of the Towers?

"Did you drink your tea and medicine?", my wife then asks. Yes, dear, I did, I answer her.

—September 11, 2001

What not to learn from the Palestinian-Israeli conflict

Always on the alert to ensure that public opinion in the United States does not start asking the wrong questions, let alone critically reassess US policy towards Israel and the Palestinian-Israeli conflict, the pro-Israel PR machine here in the United States has once again revved up with a campaign aimed at re-solidifying in the American psyche the notion that the Israeli model for dealing with terrorism is the only appropriate response to the September 11 attacks.

I say "re-solidifying" because Americans have come to accept the idea that Israel's dealing with the Palestinian resistance is the correct one without ever really hearing a rational, factually sustainable argument in its favor. What the pro-occupation forces have been fearing since September 11, given the magnitude of the attacks, is that Americans may have been shocked into awakening from their spell and may actually have begun to ask themselves and their leaders some very basic questions. The task of the pro-occupation machine, then—and it is a vitally important task—is to make sure that any stirrings towards critical reassessment of those policies are nipped in the bud and any attempt at rationally opening a debate shut down at once.

For instance, former Israeli Prime Minister Benjamin Netanyahu, who excels in this kind of shrinking the debate envelope, has been out in full force, repeating his usual platitudes and bromides about terror and terrorism, and egging on the US to unleash death and hellfire on anything and anyone who does not march to the American drum beat. Henry Kissinger is another: every time the notion is raised that perhaps the US should reassess its shortsighted policies, Kissinger becomes indignant and furiously fires back that there is no explaining evil and that we should answer fire with fire. That is, every time an attempt at going beyond the polemics of war is made, the debate is closed before it really opens, and the focus is immediately redirected at "terrorism" and the need to "eradicate it" with "merciless force". No alternatives are even deemed worthy to entertain—a clear measure of how much respect Netanyahu, Kissinger, and the like, have for democracy and the intelligence of the American public.

But rational debate and simple common sense lead us to draw conclusions that are totally opposite to those Netanyahu, Kissinger, and their various cohorts, have been desperately trying to foist on us as obvious givens. If we look at Israel's handling of terrorism, we simply cannot avoid concluding that Israel offers us not a model of what the US should do, but a model of what the US should NOT do. Israel has been fighting terrorism for decades, and yet, it remains unable to stop suicide bombers from wrecking havoc at the heart of major cities such as Tel Aviv and Jerusalem. As is well known, (a) Israel has one of the best internal and external intelligence and security agencies in the world; (b) the Palestinians it is trying to contain and neutralize are confined within a very small geographic region; (c) those Palestinians have been infiltrated inside out; (d) those same Palestinians have very limited resources; and (e) Israel has been doing this for more than fifty years;—and yet, with all that, Israel has failed, time again, in its attempt to eradicate terrorism once and for all. On the contrary, every time it has hit hard against the Palestinians—via home demolitions, assassinations, land confiscations—the result has been an escalation in violence. What makes the US think that it will be able to do better, especially given that the battle it will be waging will be world wide, across hundreds of sovereign nations, against an opponent that is sophisticated, well-financed, well-organized, highly elusive, and determined beyond comprehension?

If we are to look at the Palestinian-Israeli conflict to learn what to do, the following simple fact tells it all: between 1993 and 2000, about 400 Israelis were killed in various terrorist operations (during that same period, 3,000 Palestinians were killed by the occupation forces). The one span of time within those seven years when terrorist attacks sharply fell to almost zero was the period between Ehud Barak's election and the outbreak of the Intifada. That was a period when Palestinians saw for the first time the possibility of real independence from Israel's ruthless occupation. During that period, the Palestinian Authority found itself able to harness the political capital it had suddenly acquired with Barak's election, moving to build with its Israeli counterpart a partnership that was to lead to real co-existence. In other words, one small serious opening toward the opposition did what fifty years of sophisticated, expensive, highly intrusive, morally corrosive, security and military operations miserably failed to do.

There is a great lesson here for us to learn, if we are willing, and if are given a chance to offer the question to open and rational discussion. It is high time that one of America's most sensitive areas of foreign policy is thrown to public debate and scrutiny. God knows we don't need and can't afford to listen to the pundits and foolishly replicate Israel's costly failures on a global scale.

—September 25, 2001

Keep off the children

At the end of his first press conference, exactly one month after the tragedies of September 11th, President Bush called on America's children to send one dollar to help impoverished Afghani children fight hunger and starvation. The call, a blunt propaganda ploy aimed at wining the hearts and minds of the American people more than at alleviating the suffering of Afghani children, was hailed by the usual file of pundits and talking heads as a brilliant PR move that was sure to soften the hearts of angry Muslims, proving thus that the war campaign against Afghanistan is not a war against Islam but a war against terrorism.

The proposition that Arabs and Muslims would be duped by such a ploy—and other equally crude tricks, such as the dropping of packets of food—is sure to rankle the sensitivities of those same Arabs and Muslims. For them, Bush's call to show compassion to Afghani children will most certainly ring hypocritical, self-serving, and even shockingly exploitative. After all, a standing grievance that Arabs and Muslims, and indeed most of the world outside the US government, have held is the decade-plus long embargo on Iraq and the cruel and needless suffering it has caused Iraqi children. Indeed, according to the World Health Organization, "each month 5,000 to 6,000 children die as a result of the sanctions." UNICEF concurs by writing, "in the heavily-populated southern and central parts of the country, children under five are dying at more than twice the rate they were 10 years ago. If the substantial reduction in child mortality throughout Iraq during the 1980s had continued through the 1990s, there would have been half a million fewer deaths of children under five from 1991 to 1998."

Mr. Bush's call for compassion to starving Afghani children must have sounded hypocritical to Arabs and Muslims for a second reason: the plight of Palestinian children under occupation. Since the outbreak of the Intifada, 174 Palestinian children, dozens of them toddlers and infants, have been killed by live ammunition discharged by the occupying Israeli Defense forces, with the political, financial, and most flagrantly, military backing of the United States. In addition to the killed, tens of thousands of Palestinian children have been maimed for life, with more than half of the injuries sustained in the upper part of the body. In its crackdown on Palestinian resistance, Israel has used US-supplied anti-tank missiles, helicopter gun-ships, and snipers. And it has used them on civilian targets, causing the death of more than 700 Palestinians—more than 80% of them civilians uninvolved in the Intifada. Most scandalous—yet never an issue raised by any branch of the US government, let alone the White House—the majority of the children killed were innocent bystanders, uninvolved in any protest, with dozens of the killed struck while INSIDE their own homes by flying bullets and mortar shells fired by Israeli soldiers on densely populated areas.

How has the United States reacted to these atrocities? Has either President Clinton or President Bush rallied American children to show compassion for Palestinian children? Hardly. Instead, in October 2000, only weeks into the second Intifada, when Israel's use of firepower against stone throwing civilians elicited loud outcries from the United Nations, Unicef, and all major human right organizations, the US supplied Israel with an additional 35 Black Hawk military helicopters, the very helicopters used against stone throwing Palestinian teenagers; then a few months later, in February 2001, Boeing delivered 9 Apache attack helicopters, also used against civilians. Of course, both such deliveries were patent violations of section 4 of the Arms Export Control Act, which stipulates that U.S. arms may only be used for the purposes of "legitimate self-defense" (unless one is willing to dilute the term "self-defense" to mean nothing specific). And yet, US complicity in the killing of children persists, unflinching. As reported by Israel's Ha'aretez on September 26, 2001, the United States has decided that "[US] military aid [to Israel] is to increase by $60 million annually" for at least the next ten years.

And Arabs and Muslims must not have been the only ones detecting the exploitative hypocrisy. Cuban children, under the absurd four-decade long US embargo, have also suffered greatly. Here is an excerpt from the American Association of world Health (AAWH)'s Summary Report on The Impact of U.S. Embargo on Health of Cuban People: "AAWH visited a Cuban pediatric ward then on its 22nd day without the nausea-preventing drugs normally used in chemotherapy. The 35 children in the ward were vomiting an average of 28-30 times a day. Cuban children with lymphoblastic leukemia are denied access to new life-prolonging drugs, such as Oncaspar, patented by a U.S. company, that produces longer periods of remission and is less traumatic to the child patient, requiring only one sixth the number of injections. Left untreated, this type of leukemia is fatal in two to three months."[1]

President Bush spoke of evil and good, of hatred and compassion, insisting more than once that "we are good people". His call on America's children to help Afghani children was clearly meant to help us concretely assert our collective goodness, allay some of our guilt, and generally make us feel good about ourselves. But Mr. Bush will not trick anyone, least of all his own fellow Americans, and least of all America's children, into feeling good if we pick and choose which children are worthy of our compassion and which are not. To be sure, Mr. Bush's distinction between the enemy that must be fought and the innocent that could be hurt in that fight is legitimate. But the distinction must be one based on moral principles, and therefore applicable no matter where the children are from, rather than on strategic exigencies. Anything less is a cruel, cynical exploitation of innocent children on both sides.

—October 18, 2001 (The Atlanta Journal Constitution)

Seven sins and twelve key events

The prevailing consensus these days here in the United States is that Osama bin Laden speaks neither for Islam nor for the overwhelming majority of peace-loving Muslims all over the world. Bin Laden's messianic call for a clash between the faithful and the infidels, we are told, is an aberration, while the version of Islam he offers the world is a travesty that does gross violence to a peaceful religion.

The prevailing consensus, for once, has it right. However, the fact that bin Laden represents neither the faith he claims to be defending nor the Muslims he presumes to speak for, should not blind us to another basic reality: Osama bin Laden's list of grievances and the worldview within which those grievances are articulated, are not necessarily seen by Arabs and Muslims around the world as aberrations or as the ranting and raving of a mad man. Not one of the grievances bin Laden articulates, for instance, would meet with disagreement from Arabs and Muslims—Palestine, Iraq, the presence of US forces in Saudi Arabia—while the worldview within which America is viewed as an unprincipled superpower, craven when push comes to shove, treacherous to erstwhile friends, hypocritical and self-serving when it comes to human rights and democracy, is a longstanding, well-entrenched worldview common not only among fundamentalists, but also among educated, religiously uninvolved Arabs and Muslims from Morocco to Indonesia and beyond.

To understand why bin Laden's appeal and the reach of his message are much deeper than we are led to believe, we must try to understand the worldview from which bin Laden and his followers are waging their Jihaad. Within that worldview, America is guilty of seven moral failings: (1) its hypocrisy over democracy, (2) its violation of basic human rights, (3) its selective invocation of international law, (4) its support of the Israeli occupation and its unwillingness to exert pressure on Israel, (5) its commitment to keeping Muslims weak and divided, (6) its unreliability as a partner in a fight, and (7) its unwillingness to withstand suffering.

Perhaps the best way to grasp the essence of this worldview is to highlight the importance, in the minds of most Arabs and Muslims around the world, of the following key historical episodes:

(1) The use of atomic bombs in Hiroshima and Nagasaki: this event is viewed as a vivid illustration of American disregard for innocent lives and the clearest proof of American hypocrisy over human rights and international law;

(2) The 1953 overthrow of the democratically elected government of Mossadeq in Iran: time and again, this CIA/MIA operation is pointed out in sermons and in pamphlets as solid proof that America and the West in general are not principally committed to democracy;

(3) The 1973 October war between Israel and the Arabs: this episode is viewed as proof that Israel could never survive without the help of the United States—the consensus among Arabs and Muslims being that Israel was on the brink of defeat had the United States not intervened;

(4) The hasty retreat of the United States from Vietnam: this episode is considered as a vivid illustration of how the United States is willing to let its closest allies down when push comes to shove;

(5) The 1980-1988 Iran-Iraq war: viewed as a war fueled and maintained by the United States, Europe and Israel—the consensus within the Arab and Muslim worlds is that the US fed the Iraqis while Europe and Israel fed the Iranians: hence the conclusion that Christians and Jews were laboring to ensure a perpetual emasculation of Muslims;

(6) The September 16-18, 1982 Sabra and Shatila massacres and America's silence over them: this is viewed as proof of American hypocrisy over human rights; the March 16, 1988, gassing by Saddam Hussein—then an ally of the United States in Iraq's war against Iran—of Kurdish civilians in the village of Halabjeh, killing an estimated 5,000 villagers and injuring another 10,000, and America's silence over the atrocity, are also viewed as a vivid illustration of American hypocrisy over human rights and international law;

(7) The Gulf war and the killing of tens of thousands of Iraqi civilians in the name of repelling occupation: this episode, when contrasted to the Israeli occupation, is considered as further proof of blatant American hypocrisy and selective application of international law;

(8) The 1991 clash between the Bush administration and Israel: the perception is that the United States, when it wants to, can exert pressure on Israel to force it to sit down and negotiate a settlement with the Palestinians;

(9) The Gulf war and how the US abandoned the rebellious Kurdish and Shiite populations: proof that, as in Vietnam, the US is not a principled partner, and that for all its might, the US lacks basic moral courage;

(10) The 1995 arms embargo against Bosnia: viewed as a Euro-American conspiracy to ensure that a viable Muslim Bosnia does not take hold within Europe;

(11) The 1996 Somalia debacle: America's hasty retreat is viewed once again as an illustration of how the mighty giant will flinch at the slightest discomfort;

(12) Ariel Sharon's assertion, in September 2000, that the Temple Mount/Al-Haram is sovereign Israeli territory: the episode is viewed, at least partially, in religious terms as yet the latest assault against Muslims by Jews and Christians;

America perceives itself primarily in moral terms and prides itself for standing on the side of right and good. A large portion of the world views America in nearly opposite terms. That is why, unlike a Charles Manson or a David Koresh—whose outlandish, doomsday fantasies kept their appeal well contained within a miniscule fringe—Osama bin Laden's grievances and the worldview from which he perceives the United States—even while his violent methods and his call for a religious Jihaad are rejected—do have an echo among mainstream Arabs and Muslims around the world. Unless the United States is willing to fully and soberly understand how it is perceived by a large segment of the outside world, its current "war against terrorism" will simply end up as yet another flare up, yet another historical milestone, yet another instance of what is viewed as America's long list of moral failures.

—October 19, 2001

If the CIA had butted out.....

Imagine if August 19, 1953, had come and gone, uneventfully. Imagine if Operation Ajax, coordinated by the British MI6 and the American CIA, which toppled the flourishing democracy in Iran of Mohammed Mossadeq, had never left the drawing board. Imagine if the Western-educated Mossadeq, a charismatic leader who was massively backed in Iran by a burgeoning middle class, had been allowed to peacefully lead his country to become the first truly Muslim democracy in the Middle East.

And imagine if his government had been allowed to assume its obligations and responsibilities, as stipulated by the 1906 constitution, and if the shah had been allowed to reign but not rule, as again stipulated by the Iranian constitution, and imagine if Britain and the United States had not been egged on by oil companies livid over Mossadeq's nationalization of oil interests in Iran but instead had stayed out of Iran's business and not intervened. Imagine what would have likely happened.

Had the coup never taken place, Iran probably would have gone on to build a sturdy, inclusive democracy that would have brought about a far more durable stability than what the shah—forever tainted in the eyes of his people as a weak, easily manipulated Western puppet—ever managed to deliver. Had the coup never taken place, democratic Iran would have long ago done away with the myth that Islam and democracy are incompatible. More important, nationalist and anti-colonialist as it was, Iran would have handsomely served as the model to follow for the dozens of Arab and Muslim states that had recently gained, or were about to gain, independence from colonial occupation, thus averting their alignment with the Soviet bloc as well as the rise of home-grown thugs and dictators.

Had the coup never taken place, the ayatollahs, who had supported the coup against Mossadeq, would never have gained their political clout. Indeed, the shah saw in the conservative ayatollahs the perfect partners against the radicalism of the left and the liberalism of the middle class.

Had the coup never taken place and the ayatollahs never been given the political clout they had enjoyed under the shah, the June uprising of 1963, which was fueled by the clerics' unhappiness with the shah's attempts at modernization, would also have never taken place. Hence no harsh crackdown would have followed the uprising, and a little-known cleric, a certain Ayatollah Ruhollah Khomeini, would not have gained international attention as the spiritual leader of that confrontation against the shah.

Had the coup never taken place, Khomeini would have remained a little-known cleric. Instead, he was exiled for 14 years, a time during which he cultivated his image from that of a charismatic leader to that of a sacred returning messiah. And during those 14 years, the prospect for the emergence of a truly democratic Iran grew dimmer while Islamic radicalism, associating all that is Western with the hated shah and his supporters—principally the United States—took a deeper hold on the passions of an increasingly frustrated younger generation.

Had the coup never taken place, there would not have been a hostage crisis, and the United States would not have severed its relations with Iran and imposed economic sanctions. Both actions, more than 20 years later, remain in effect to this day.

Had the coup never taken place, Saddam Hussein would have never dared invade Iran in September 1980. The United States would never have sided with Iraq's dictator and neither would it have committed itself to a policy of ensuring that Iraq not lose the war. It would not have supplied Hussein with crucial assistance or turned a blind eye to his egregious crimes against his people.

Had the cup never taken place, Hussein would not have found himself by the end of the war against Iran as the commander of one of the largest armies in the Middle East. More important, he would have never been under the impression that, as long as he restricted his aggression to fellow Muslims and kept off Israel, the world would only decry and condemn him but never act.

Had the coup never taken place, chances are that Iraq never would have invaded Kuwait, and the United States never would have had to orchestrate a massive military campaign against his army, let alone establish bases on Saudi soil. It would not have rendered talk about human rights and international law totally meaningless and hypocritical to Arab and Muslim ears.

Imagine a new era of foreign policy—an era in which international law is taken seriously, respected, in which sovereign democracies are encouraged, nurt-ured, applauded, rather than fought against, stifled and killed.

Imagine if we abandoned, once and for all the poisonous doctrines of "Iron Chancellor" Bismarck and Henry Kissinger and instead subscribed to those of Amnesty International and Human Rights Watch.

Imagine if we took the United Nations and The Hague seriously, rather than treating them as kangaroo courts in which only those causes championed by the mighty and powerful were pursued with vigor, while other grievances were neglected and scorned. How many millions of lives would we have saved, and how much safer and more prosperous would the world be today?

—October 21, 2001 (The Los Angeles Times)

America since 9/11

Remember what we were talking about just before September 11? Let me remind you: shark attacks and Gary Condit. Indeed, I remember vividly how Wolf Blitzer of CNN, after being told (not for the first time) by one of the shark experts he was interviewing that, in fact, this year the number of shark attacks was lower than an average year, turned to us and urgently asked the burning question: "but how concerned should the general public be and is the media hyping the story too much?" Had 911 never taken place, Blitzer—the shark season irretrievably over—would now have been burrowing deep into Condit, his fangs well ensconced, not to mention the resurrection of OJ and his road rage trial. It would have been great to see what Ito has been up to these days....

Ah, but now Collin Quinn of Saturday Night Live takes a jibe at Noam Chomsky, while NPR's Terry Gross devotes a whole hour on the Egyptian Islamic thinker Sayyid Qutb. [2] A whiff of sophistication and depth, dare I say?

For those who might have been taken in by the slogan "compassionate conservative" and may have been still wondering what the Bush administration was all about, note and remember this: the very first instinct the Bush administration had just after the attacks and while the nation was still reeling from the shock, was to wonder how many billions of dollars to put together to bail out the airline industry. It was not: how do we take care of the victims and their relatives—they had to organize their own concerts and benefits.

And so it turns out, after all, that the free market is not the best means for achieving safety. It turns out, in fact, that the free market gives you only the cheapest safety system you can buy—and hence, the worst—given that the balancing act is between human life on the one hand and profits and profit margins on the other. And guess where the balance will always tip...And so, the strongest believers in free enterprise were the first to bang on the door of the despised Federal Government—and bang to demand two things: one, bail us out by giving us some free money, and two, please pay for whatever it takes to make the skies friendlier and safer again.

And then there is the Déjà vu: Remember Bush Senior, Jim Baker, Cheney and Powell, back in '90 and '91? Remember how they insisted on no negotiations with Saddam, ever, even if it meant that it could (or perhaps precisely because it could) lead to Hussein's peaceful and unconditional withdrawal from Kuwait? Remember De Cuellar and how the administration was incensed at the man for trying to establish dialog and avert mass slaughter? Annan is staying out of this one (his experience as the UN's special envoy to NATO coming in handy)—clearly he has learned that it is futile to mention reason when the US war machine has engaged.....

Americans are incredulous that anyone could have such strong hostility towards them. Are they buying the canard that people hate them because of their democracy, their freedom, their strength, their goodness even? Some are. Many are not. But with all the flags and the shouting and the anger and the hatred, only the bravest are daring to veer off the flock and ask questions. The most unscrupulous also are dissenting: the ones who call on Bush to go at it alone and to forget the coalition, to bomb Afghanistan flat, then to topple off Syria, Iran, Iraq and Libya.... Bush is wavering, and leaning—at least for now—towards "restraint", but who knows what he would do if something horrible were to take place again....

"America is quickly feeling more and more like Europe," an Algerian friend of mine told me a couple of weeks ago. He said this with great sadness, and I felt the sadness too: paradise lost. Forever? Maybe. Or maybe not. The raw quest for wealth above all is this nation's curse, but it is also its blessing—in a way. Tragedies come and go, but the mighty dollar and the freedom to chase it are here to stay. So mighty it is that a civil war that pitted brother against brother for years and did split the nation in two, could not overcome it. What a mighty principle—to throw in a saving irony.

So, let the profiteers march in: "wealth has never yet sacrificed itself on the altar of patriotism," said Robert La Follette back in WWI. Toy soldiers are taking a hit, but toy firemen and policemen are raking it. The flag business is good, also. Airplane travel is down, but trains and buses are doing better than usual. So are handguns, rifles, bullets, security systems, and anything that has to do with protecting yourself. An Anthrax home testing kit—no joke—will hit market soon, provided the scare sticks....

—October 24, 2001

Time for a stark choice: peace or Sharon

Ariel Sharon has never minced words about his long-term vision for Israel and the future he has in store for his Palestinian neighbors. Asked in an interview with the Israeli newspaper Ha'aretz back in April of this year, only a few weeks after becoming Prime Minister, "Would you be ready to evacuate settlements as part of a non-belligerency agreement?", Sharon answered bluntly: "No. Absolutely not." "Not even isolated settlements like Netzarim in the Gaza Strip?", the interviewer followed up; "No. Not at any price. Why do we have to evacuate Netzarim? For what?", Sharon answered, unwavering.

Sharon's vision is and has always been that of a Greater Israel in full control of what he calls Judea and Samaria (what the rest of the world calls the West Bank) and the Gaza Strip. Within this Greater Israel, Palestinians would be confined to "security zones" dotted by settlements and army bases, their movement closely watched and regulated, and their economy tightly controlled and subservient to that of Israel. Palestinians within this scheme would be allowed to "administer" themselves—that is, take care of the day-to-day chores of picking up garbage, sweeping the streets, regulating traffic jams and chasing common thieves—but would not under any circumstances be allowed to build an independent economy or live free from outside interference as a sovereign nation should. In other words, Ariel Sharon wants to turn the indigenous four million Palestinians that surround Israel to the equivalent of America's Natives (minus the citizenship offer): formally recognize them as forming "a nation", but recognize them as such only nominally. (It is no coincidence that the one successful business in the West Bank and Gaza before the outbreak of the second Intifada was the casino industry!)

Small wonder, then, that when President Bush stated publicly that the United States envisions, and has always envisioned, a Palestinian state as the end point of a final settlement, Ariel Sharon shot back with a bitter reference to the 1938 sellout of Czechoslovakia to the Germans—a thinly veiled charge of anti-Semitism against Israel's long-time ally, benefactor and protector. Israel should not be sacrificed for the sake of building a coalition with the Arabs, Sharon protested, drawing a "sharp rebuke" from a White House growing increasingly impatient with the unwieldy Prime Minister.

Sharon of course meant every word when he said that recognition of a Palestinian state was tantamount to sacrificing Israel. And he was right: the existence of a sovereign Palestinian state on "Judea and Samaria" means the end of what Sharon calls the "Zionist project" and the end of Israel as HE envisions it.

So, then, where does this leave the Bush administration and its Mitchell Plan, which calls for, among other things, a total freeze on any future settlement building? Nowhere. The Mitchell Plan is a non-starter as long as Ariel Sharon is in power and his Zionist vision of a Greater Israel remains alive. If the Peace Process and progress towards a final resolution to the conflict are to become reachable goals once again—as they were tantalizingly close to becoming during the last round of negotiations with Barak in Taba, a few weeks before Barak's defeat—Ariel Sharon must leave office and the Zionist project of a greater Israel must come to a close.

Back in 1991, George Bush the father, facing an unyielding Yitzhak Shamir, threatened Israel with withholding financial aid if settlement building in the Occupied Territories continued. That confrontation resulted in the convening of a conference in Madrid that included Israelis, Americans, Syrians, and other Arab representatives, along with some Palestinians who did not officially represent the PLO. For the first time ever, and after decades of stalling and detracting, attacking and then crying wolf, after years of obfuscation, Israel finally agreed to negotiate.

George Bush the son faces a similar situation now, but his opportunity is far more significant than the one created by his father's bold challenge to Yitzhak Shamir. With the Godfather of radical, expansionist Zionism at helm of Israel's government, George Bush the son has the opportunity to confront head on, and bring an end to, the very idea of expansionist Zionism.

Most Israelis, let alone Jews, are not interested in Sharon's vision of a Greater Israel; they simply want an end to the conflict and lasting, peaceful co-existence with the Palestinians.[3] They are not interested in building new settlements, but rather in building their own economy and normalizing their relation with the outside world. Ariel Sharon's priorities are exactly the opposite: he has demonstrated since he became Prime Minister that he is willing to sacrifice everything—Israel's economy, its security, and even its crucial relationship with the United States—for the sake of maintaining his project alive.

But the lesson of 1991 tells us that Israel will sacrifice everything except its special relationship with the United States. This provides George Bush with an opening to offer the Israelis a stark choice—as he knows very well how to do: either you are with us or you are with Ariel Sharon. Either give up the notion of a Greater Israel or give up support from the United States.

If Sharon falls, and especially if he does as a result of direct and open US pressure, the expansionist project—and the temptation to pursue it—will come to an end, once and for all, and peace with the Palestinians will at long last become a tangible, accessible possibility. The opportunity is here and the next step is obvious. The question is: will Bush the son dare be so bold as to emulate his father?

—November 4, 2001 (The Jordan Times)

Letter from Henry

From: Henry Kissinger
To: President George W. Bush

Dear Mr. President:

First, let me congratulate you on the excellent job you are doing in your campaign against bin Laden and the Taliban. The strategy you have adopted and the firm, unwavering manner with which you have executed it, have inspired awe and admiration even in an old, worn out cynic such as myself.

At the national level, you have bravely seized the moment and carried out a series of long-overdue reforms. Indeed, under your young stewardship, the executive is finally regaining some of the powers it undeservedly lost to, and never recovered from, an over-reaching Congress in the aftermath of the Viet Nam war and Watergate. Your bold overturn, for example, of the 1978 presidential Records Act comes at a crucial moment when it is of paramount importance that we reestablish an "orderly process" in sharing information, as your press secretary, Ari Fleischer, so succinctly put it.

Similarly, your establishment of the Home Security cabinet position—hence effectively bringing under direct executive control a dozen of agencies, including both the FBI and the CIA—is also another masterstroke. Add to this the far-reaching, wide-sweeping terrorism bill, the new provisions that all but nullify attorney-client privileges, your recent executive order that would allow the government to try people accused of terrorism in front of a special military commission instead of a civilian court, and even an old curmudgeon such as myself is starting to feel hopeful and optimistic again that at long last government can perhaps start conducting policy on rational, pragmatic grounds, protected from the hysterical shrill of misguided idealists who naively believe that this chaotic, brutish world can be ordered with laws and conventions.

Your success at the international level has been no less impressive. In your deliberate preparations for the offensive, you have managed to rally to our side not only our old friends—from the steadfast and always reliable British, to the lukewarm and unreliable French—but even our enemies, such as Syria, Libya, and China. Indeed, our old foe and nemesis Iran is clamoring to jump on the bandwagon! Moreover, our fight against the Taliban, which many warned us would be brutal and long-drawn, even disastrous, has proven to be the opposite: we've helped drive them out of Kabul in just a few weeks, and now half of Afghanistan is effectively under our control.

In other words: an all around success.

Now, as we look forward, may I offer the following piece of advice: please make sure that you do not listen to those hawks in your administration who are naively calling for the complete defeat of the Taliban and the elimination of Osama bin Laden. To be sure, defeating the Taliban and apprehending bin Laden are now tantalizingly achievable goals. But the real question we must ask ourselves is this: what are the consequences of completely wiping out the Taliban and bin Laden?

Put simply: with the Taliban gone and bin Laden liquidated, we would no longer be able to justify our presence in that most crucial region. And I can assure you that, as friendly as Russia, Pakistan, China, and the Northern Alliance are to us now, the last thing they would be willing to tolerate is an established American presence in the region.

On the other hand, if the Taliban continue to occupy southern Afghanistan, and if Osama bin Laden were to remain on the loose, then our presence would be easily justified. Just as we are doing in Iraq, with the continuing presence of our other Evil One, Saddam Hussein, we can claim that we are there to PROTECT the surrounding countries from the scourge of the Taliban and the threat of bin Laden.

Either way, I can assure you, Mr. President, that when historians look back to this war campaign, they will be awed by the meticulous planning that has gone into it. For instance, they will duly note how, drawing the right lessons from previous wars, you have learned that neutralizing criticism here at home is as important as the massive hardware at our disposal. Your food air-drops, for example, even if the Red Cross and the UN opposed them, did the trick and enabled us to continue claiming that we are a compassionate nation. (Your call on America's children to send in money to help Afghani children was a stroke of genius.) Then there is that unprecedented concession from CNN, when its chief issued an order to his journalists not to focus too much on Afghani civilian casualties, and the equally unprecedented mobilization of Hollywood's big moguls—people who once swore never to recognize you as their president—offering their services for any propaganda campaign you may wish to undertake. But best of all is your daring bombing of the Al-Jazeera facilities—hence putting them out circulation just before the Northern Alliance took over Kabul—was yet another example of a brilliant idea boldly executed. Reporters Sans Frontières can raise a dust storm if they want, but the bottom line is that Americans got to see images of Afghani men shaving their beards, Afghani women casting off their burqas, and everyone dancing to the blare of once-banned music, instead of pictures of summary executions and civilian suffering.

And last, but certainly not least, let me simply say that I highly appreciate the speed with which you are putting all of this into motion. God knows how fickle public opinion is, here and abroad. Needless to say that it heartens me to see a president willing to strike while the iron is hot.

So, Mr. President: I thank you for seizing the moment and for restoring sovereignty to those who were meant to lead and govern. The world, as always, will in the end be thankful that we did.

HK

—November 16, 2001

Why do they hate us?

"I have no doubt that civilians deserve punishment." These words were famously uttered not by Osama bin Laden after the atrocities of Sept. 11, 2001, but by the prime minister of America's closest ally, Menachem Begin, who spoke them publicly, on the record, addressing Israel's Knesset during Israel's invasion of Lebanon in June 1982. The civilians he was referring to were, of course, the millions of Palestinians living in utter destitution in refugee camps in Lebanon.

Begin's logic was simple, impeccable, airtight: since the PLO could not operate, survive, and flourish without the support it enjoyed from the Palestinian people, an important component in the strategy of breaking the back of the PLO was to raise the price of supporting it to above what regular Palestinian civilians could tolerate. This meant not only making daily life a running series of humiliations—from roadblocks that made free movement impossible to curfews that would confine whole towns and villages to their homes for days on end, to flattening houses and confiscating land—but also pushing the envelope a bit further during the invasion, and doing so systematically, as a matter of open policy. The strategy was cruelly elegant: let's relentlessly mete out collective punishment so that the masses are made to feel the pain in their very bones and eventually reach the breaking point, say "uncle" and surrender in utter defeat.

When a couple of months later, in September 1982, close to a thousand helpless Palestinians living in Beirut's Sabra and Shatila refugee camps were slaughtered by the Christian Phalangist militia, under the watch and supervision of the Israeli army (as concluded by Israel's Kahan commission), few among those who were familiar with Israel's long-standing policy of punishing civilians as a tactic and strategy for getting at the PLO were surprised. In the name of safeguarding its security, and under the unwavering protection of the United States, Israel was given carte blanche to do as it pleased, including playing with the lives of innocent civilians. And so, predictably, during its Lebanon invasion campaign, Israel killed more than 17,500 Lebanese civilians, maimed untold hundreds of thousands, and caused the utter devastation of an entire country.

Back then, a question all Palestinians, Lebanese, Arabs and Muslims repeatedly asked themselves and the world around them was: why does America hate us so much that they would not only tolerate, but finance and politically support our physical extermination in broad daylight, under the glare of cameras and the watch of journalists?

Most of the innocent lives lost on Sept. 11, 2001, were lost in a flash, in a ghastly instant, when no one could have intervened to stop the carnage. During its invasion of Lebanon, however, Israel could have been stopped, just as the Phalangists, taking long hours to carry out their dastardly deed, could have been stopped. To this day, Palestinians and Lebanese ask, never really recovering from that nightmare: why didn't the United States, lover of humanity, intervene to stop the horrors?

Twenty years later, the same questions are being asked about the current uprising in the occupied territories: why does the mightiest nation in the world, the purported lover and defender of peace and human dignity, not only stand on the sidelines, but provide military and financial aid to an ally and beneficiary that continues practicing its decades-long policy of blockading whole populations, demolishing houses, confiscating land, tearing up roads, using live ammunition against stone-throwers, and assassinating, as a matter of open policy, the popular leadership of the Palestinian people?

Americans watched in dismay as some Palestinians "cheered" the news of the attack on the World Trade Center. They watched and asked in horror: why do they hate us so much? But Americans must remember that they too "celebrated" when Baghdad went up in flames, 10 years ago. They rallied, tied yellow ribbons, and turned on their headlights, as their mighty navy and air force visited horror and death upon the innocent, to the tune of more than 10,000 civilians killed during the five-week air campaign alone. Hundreds of thousands later would die an agonizing, slow death, from disease directly caused by the destruction of Baghdad's sewage system. Iraqis watching the reaction of Americans must have wondered why anyone—and especially a people living in prosperity and under the protection of a mighty military force, and oceans away—would celebrate the killing of helpless civilians sitting terrified in their dark homes while hundreds of jet fighters dropped bombs on their city—and celebrate not once, or twice, but day in and day out, for five weeks of round-the-clock bombing.

And they continue to ask, to this day: why do Americans hate us so much that they would insist on imposing a decade-long embargo that has done nothing but ensure the misery of ordinary civilians, costing the lives of half a million of our children, devastating thus a whole generation of Iraqis, and reducing what was once far and ahead the most modern Arab country to a backward nation barely able to subsist? Why?

—December 1, 2001 (The Washington Report on Middle East Affairs)

Yes: Israelis can stop cycle of violence with negotiations, not provocations

In a gripping October Harper's article, New York Times reporter Christopher Hedges described how every afternoon around four o'clock at the outskirts of the Khan Yunis refugee camp, a voice on a loud speaker is heard spewing out insults in Arabic, calling out, "Come on, dogs!...Son of a whore!"[4]

To his astonishment, Hedges discovered that the loud speakers were mounted on armored Israeli vehicles. Soon after, riled by the invectives, young Palestinian boys, most of them no more than 10 or 11 years old, would dash toward the armored vehicles and begin throwing rocks at the soldiers. At which point, the soldiers would open fire.

To Americans, the notion that Israel would go out of its way to provoke and incite Palestinians, let alone Palestinian children, to violence is beyond belief.

And yet, evidence is abundant that Israel is not engaged in self-defense—certainly not as it is understood under international law—but rather in deliberate provocation aimed at creating an unstable atmosphere within which Israel can undertake its military operations with impunity.

Let's revisit the few weeks before the tragic Dec. 1 and 2 bombings in Jerusalem and Tel Aviv. Nov. 7: the Red Crescent reports that Israeli Defense Force (IDF) soldiers shoot in cold blood three wounded Palestinian gunmen under their custody after medics were unable to save the life of a wounded Israeli soldier; Nov. 13: The Israeli human rights group B'tselem uncovers that the IDF has a policy of not prosecuting Israeli soldiers who have shot and killed, without provocation, Palestinian children; Nov. 22: Five boys are killed when an ordnance planted by the IDF deep into civilian Palestinian territory explodes; Nov. 23: Four Palestinians are killed during the boys' funeral march, among them a 14-year-old boy.

But what ignited this latest firestorm is of course the Nov. 23 assassination of military Hamas leader Mahmoud Abu Hanoud. As expected, Hamas vowed revenge. And so there was.

Did Israel expect such a reaction? Of course it did. It knew full well that just as the taunted children of Gaza throw rocks at their tormenting soldiers, so do Hamas and Islamic Jihad, taunted by assassinations, bombings of densely populated areas, house demolitions and land confiscations, react with their weapon of choice: suicide bombings.

Why would Israel engage in such provocations?

As demonstrated by Camp David, the Palestinians are not willing to settle for anything less than a sovereign Palestinian state, and the Israelis are not willing to offer anything resembling a sovereign Palestinian state. The Palestinians, militarily no match for the Israelis, have time and again pleaded for an unconditional return to the negotiation table.

The Israelis have decided that negotiations are a dead end for attaining their goal of a semi-autonomous Palestinian state and have instead opted for the time-tested strategy of divide and conquer: Establish a state of chaos, so Israel is no longer faced with solving a political problem, but rather with confronting a security crisis, and then tighten control over the remaining Palestinian territories.

In this light, it becomes perfectly clear why the Israelis are making it virtually impossible—not only politically, but now physically—for Yasir Arafat to bring about order among his people.

Between 1993 and 2000, about 400 Israelis were killed in militant Palestinian actions (3,000 were felled on the Palestinian side). The only period during that interval when Israeli fatalities fell to almost zero was during the last year under Ehud Barak, when Palestinians truly believed their ordeal was at an end.

The cycle of violence will be broken only if and when Israel abandons its tactics of provocation and collective punishment and realizes there is no alternative to creating a free, sovereign Palestinian state.

—December 9, 1001 (The Detroit News)

Israel's strategy: sparking a Palestinian civil war

Those who intimately follow the Israeli media know that Alex Fishman, the security commentator for Yediot Achronot, Israel's largest circulation mass newspaper, is no soft dove. Reflecting the overwrought, frustrated mood of most Israelis, Fishman has been a solid supporter of Sharon's policy of assassination from day one. And yet, two days following the assassination of Hamas leader Mahmud Abu Hunud, and one week before the suicide bombings of Jerusalem and Haifa, Fishman denounced the killing of Hanud as "a dangerous liquidation".

He wrote in his commentary—which was given a very conspicuous place, in a box on the paper's front page—that, "whoever gave a green light to this act of liquidation knew full well that he is thereby shattering in one blow the gentleman's agreement between Hamas and the Palestinian Authority; under that agreement, Hamas was to avoid in the near future suicide bombings inside the Green Line, of the kind perpetrated at the Dolphinarium [discotheque in Tel-Aviv]." Predicting what was to follow with deadly accuracy, Fishman wrote, "we again find ourselves preparing with dread for a new mass terrorist attack within the Green Line [Israel's pre-'67 border]".

Fishman then goes on to ask: "But does this string of operational successes serve any political aim, any strategy leading anywhere? Do 20 liquidations or 50 make any substantial difference, either in the campaign against terrorism or in the political arena?"

Fishman asks his question rhetorically and simply to illustrate what he believes is the 'irrationality' of Sharon's actions. But let us take the question seriously: could Ariel Sharon perhaps be acting rationally, after all, deliberately, within the framework of his own long-term agenda?

Some basic observations are in order.

If Ariel Sharon's motivation were only to press Arafat to reign in radical militants, then why does he make it politically—and now physically—impossible for him to do so, by humiliating him, denouncing him as the bin Laden of Israel, and physically dismantling his security apparatus and the infrastructure of his authority? As Fishman notes, Arafat was relatively successful in reigning in Hamas during the months preceding the assassination, and had even begun arresting some Hamas activists. Why then did Sharon engage in an action he knew full well would only destroy any fragile balance Arafat was slowly building with the militants?

A second observation: Israel has been 'cracking down' on terrorism for three decades now, and yet to this day suicide bombings continue to take place. Under Sharon, as Fishman observes, "the number of "special operations" in the Gaza Strip—i.e., secret penetrations into the [Palestinian-controlled] 'A' area for the purpose of prevention, arrests, ambushes and liquidations—has arisen by 400% in the past three months." And yet, Israel is now reeling from the most horrific string of suicide bombings against Israeli civilians since 1996. If Sharon is, as he must be, well aware that "cracking down" on terrorism has never succeeded in bringing the violence down, but only in increasing it, then why does he continue to pursue that deadly policy?

A third observation: Ariel Sharon has never minced words about his long-term vision for Israel and the future he has in store for his Palestinian neighbors. Asked in an interview with the Israeli newspaper Ha'aretz back in April of this year, only a few weeks after becoming Prime Minister, "Would you be ready to evacuate settlements as part of a non-belligerency agreement?", Sharon answered bluntly: "No. Absolutely not."

"Not even isolated settlements like Netzarim in the Gaza Strip?", the interviewer followed up; "No. Not at any price," Sharon answered. "Why do we have to evacuate Netzarim? For what?"

And fourth: between 1993 and 2000, a period during which Israel was expected to withdraw from the occupied territories, the size of Israeli settlements and the population that came with it doubled. If Israel were truly serious about ending the occupation, then why did its occupation expand and not retract?

Given these realities, let us go back to Fishman's rhetorical question: "But does this string of operational successes serve any political aim, any strategy leading anywhere?"

The answer is a resounding, 'yes.'

As demonstrated by Camp David, the Palestinians are not willing to settle for anything less than a sovereign Palestinian state, and the Israelis are not willing to offer anything resembling a sovereign Palestinian state. The Palestinians, militarily no match for the Israelis, have time and again pleaded for an unconditional return to the negotiation table. The Israelis, holding the military upper hand, have decided that negotiations are a dead end for attaining their goal of a semi-autonomous, physically dismembered, Bantustans-cum-Palestinian state, and have instead opted for the time-tested strategy of divide and conquer: spread civil strife among the Palestinians, establish a state of chaos, so that Israel is no longer faced with solving a political problem, but rather with confronting a security crisis, and then move in to further dismember, annex, and tighten control over the remaining Palestinian territories. The maps since 1947 tell the whole story so far, and the story has yet to change.

—December 21, 2001 (EuropaWorld)

Watching a fire across the river

As widely reported in the American and Israeli press at the time, on July 10, 2000, just before boarding his plane for Camp David, then Prime Minister Ehud Barak enunciated three "red lines" which he promised he would never cross under any circumstances. First was the red line of Jerusalem: Barak solemnly pledged that Jerusalem would remain fully united under Israeli sovereignty; second was the red line of the settlements: the majority of the settlers of "Judea and Samaria" (the West Bank), Barak promised, would be in settlement blocs under full Israeli sovereignty; and third was the red line of Palestinian refugees' right of return: not only would Israel refuse to accept any moral responsibility for the Palestinian tragedy, but would under no circumstances allow Palestinians to return to their homes.

In addition to these "red lines", Barak also promised the following: a separation between Israel and the Palestinians and no return to the 1967 lines.

As also widely reported at the time, Yasir Arafat warned both Mr. Barak and then president Bill Clinton that ground-work for a final settlement was far from complete and that the time was still not ripe for a final, permanent status to be signed. "If I sign this document," Arafat is famously reported to have said to both Barak and Clinton, "would you walk in my funeral?" But both Barak, and Clinton by his side, insisted that the talks be held, in the lime light, committing thus one of the most basic mistakes in international diplomacy: raising expectations to such a fever pitch that no matter how successful the talks could have been, they would never have met those expectations and thus could never have been deemed a success.

But did Barak really make a "mistake", or was Camp David and the unreasonable expectations built up around it, a calculated move?

When Yasir Arafat returned from Camp David, having refused to be brow beaten to a signature, he was welcomed back by his people as a true hero who had stood up for his people's rights—a first in a whole decade perhaps for a man against

whom a reservoir of anger and contempt had been steadily building from a population that was now far worse off than it had been at the start of the "peace process" back in 1993. Everyone was well aware of the tremendous pressure exerted
on Arafat by a Bill Clinton anxious to clinch something from the claws of history
for the legacy of his fading presidency, and Palestinians heaved a heavy sigh of
relief when Arafat resisted.

Barak and the Israelis were of course fully aware of all of this: whatever deal
Arafat and the Palestinian Authority may have signed in Camp David, given
Israel's "read lines", would have been rejected by the population on the ground as
null and void.

But Barak, with president Clinton's full backing, insisted that either Arafat close
the deal, or the talks be publicly declared as a failure. And so, rather than
announce, as any attempts at serious negotiations that hit a snag do, that the talks
were frank, that no agreement had yet been reached, but that the two sides would
continue to talk, and immediately schedule another round of negotiations, president Clinton went on international Television and announced to an anxious
world and a Middle East on edge, that "the talks had failed". No follow up talks
were scheduled.

Hence plan A was shelved—at least for the time being—and Plan B kicked in.

And what was plan A?

When we hear of Barak's "generous concessions", we almost never hear of the
concessions from the Palestinian side. Beside conceding half of the territory to
which they are entitled under the 1947 Partition Plan (the famous 97% offered
by Barak apply to less than half of that territory), the Palestinians were asked to
take a radical step forward: renounce all claims against the state of Israel. But
given Barak's "red lines" and the rejection of the Palestinian people of any deal
that would have called on them to renounce their claims without full Palestinian
sovereignty over the future Palestinian state and without the complete withdrawal
of Israel from Palestinian land, no one who is seriously familiar with the conflict
would have expected that any such deal signed by Arafat would lead to anything
but another cycle of violence in the conflict.

The difference being, of course, that a state under attack from elements of a
neighboring, even if nominally sovereign, state, would have the full backing of

international law and the United Nations in its attempts to react to such violence.

In other words, the purpose of plan A is to eliminate the only remaining weapon the weak and dispossessed Palestinians have on their side: the moral high ground and international law.

And so, plan B kicked in. Immediately following the collapse of Camp David, Barak unleashes the specter of Ariel Sharon against Arafat by allowing him (in fact, helping him with 1,000 body guards) to "visit" the Haram-Al-Sharif/Temple Mount and assert that the Temple, and Jerusalem in its entirely, is and will always be under Israeli sovereignty. Then, when the Palestinians react as fully expected, Barak opens fire against stone throwers, killing seven protesters on the very first day of the uprising, mostly teenagers, and injuring hundreds. Funerals follow, more stone throwing, and Barak's army continues to open fire, aiming to kill and maim, rather than control and diffuse, as Amnesty International and Human Rights Watch have detailed in numerous reports on the reaction of the IDF in the months that followed. And all along, Barak's demand is unwavering: "the violence" must end, Arafat must stop his people from throwing stones at the well-shielded, well-equipped, armed-to-the-teeth, Israeli army.

And so the months pass, and with the killing of more Palestinian stone throwers, hundreds of civilians—two hundred of whom are children, dozens toddlers killed near or INSIDE their homes by indiscriminate Israeli shelling of Palestinian civilian areas—Palestinian resistance graduates from stone throwing, to mortar attacks, to suicide bombings. And with every Palestinian reaction, Israel "retaliates" with more shooting, more bombing, more home demolitions, and more assassinations of Palestinian leaders.

And so, from Ehud Barak's nebulously impossible demand that "Arafat stop the violence" against army outposts, all while Israel continues to react with far greater deadly violence against civilians, now we have Ariel Sharon's well-attuned-to-the-times demand that "Arafat 'crack down' on terrorists." But in either case, the aim was the same: crack the strong unity that had brought the Palestinians together after Camp David and push the Palestinians to a internal civil war.

In other words, the purpose of plan B is to incite Palestinians to react violently, demand that Arafat and his Authority stop such violence, denounce Arafat for failing to achieve the impossible, threaten his physical removal given the failure, watch him fight for his survival by cracking down on his people, sit back and let inter-Palestinian strife build steam, and then, when all hell breaks loose, move in, reoccupy more territory in the name of restoring order and ensuring Israeli security.

Ultimately Israel will return to the negotiating table: Plan A offers such a compelling prize—a moral level ground with the Palestinians—that it is hard to imagine anyone in mainstream Israel (excepting perhaps Sharon and the hard-line settler movement) wise enough to abandon it for an equitable, truly permanent resolution that would satisfy both the Palestinian people and Israel's security concerns.

But until plans to perpetuate occupation by other—cheaper and seemingly less immoral—means are scrapped by Israel once and for all, we can all look forward to decades of more Israeli aggression and more Palestinian resistance, and more bloodshed from both sides.

—December 24, 2001

Hate speech, served raw

On Christmas eve, as the Christian world prepared for solemn mass celebrating the second millennial birth day of Jesus Christ, I had the ugly misfortune of catching a glimpse of the unbridled hate speech and incitement against Arabs and Muslims, and anyone who has the misfortune to look like a caricature of Arabs and Muslims, would have to suffer, once again, should another disaster at the scale of September 11 be perpetrated by yet another crazed fanatic acting in the name of an Islam disfigured beyond recognition. This happened when I accidentally tuned my radio to 1210 am, WPHT, a Philadelphia area talk station, and caught Host Bill Maar saying: "Let's face it, people, the problem is Islam itself. I'm just sick and tired of watching President Bush, Tom Daschle, and Tony Blair running around making excuses and saying that this has nothing to do with Islam. Of course it does." He then went on to say, not mincing his words: "Islam's Holy Book, the Quran [is] a terrorist manual."

Maar's comments came in reaction to the close call of December 22, when a man holding a British passport under the name of Richard C. Reid allegedly tried to detonate a bomb he had stuffed in the soles of his shoes. When Maar made his comments, rumor had it that he was perhaps a Sri-Lankan named Tariq Raja.

And Hence Maar's tirade against Islam.

It is almost a waste of time to counter Mr. Maar's lunatic ranting against a whole religion, except that it still does shock me, every single time, to discover that otherwise respectable radio stations would tolerate such raw hate speech against Islam (and ONLY against Islam, by the way) to go on the air, unchallenged. Mr. Maar's violent expressions of hatred against Islam will probably cause not a few already angry and confused Americans somewhere to at least glare angrily and hatefully at an innocent Middle-East looking bearded man, or at a scarf wearing Muslim woman; and should another disaster befall us, a few of those hateful glares will most certainly translate to an ugly, tragic act. Where will Mr. Maar be when a mother, or a sister, or a brother, or a son, or a daughter, loses a loved one because some angry American "fed up with coddling Islam" decides that it's time to sound a wake up call to all the Arabs and Muslims of America?

But I will try to counter the unconscionable, if for no other reason than to make sure that no one ever thinks that such irresponsible hate speech goes unnoticed by us Muslims here in the United States.

Maar declares Islam to be a violent religion by making two points: (1) he cites the Qur'an itself as being a book laced with incitements to kill the infidels, and (2) he points out that all of the people who are wishing us (read "red blooded Americans") harm are Muslim.

To the charge against the Holy book, perhaps Mr. Maar would like to apply that same charge against both the Old and the New Testaments, since they too are "laced" with incitement to violence against the non-believers.

In the Old Testament, we read: "Their children also shall be dashed to pieces before their eyes; their houses shall be spoiled and their wives ravished." (Isaiah 13:16) And later "...and they shall have no pity on the fruit of the womb; their eye shall not spare children." (Isaiah 13:18) We also read, one: "Then Menahem smote Tiphsah, and all that were therein, and the coasts thereof from Tirzah: because they opened not to him, therefore he smote it; and all the women therein that were with child he ripped up." (2 Kings 15:16) And I have a long list of such violent language.

In the New Testament we read Jesus Christ himself saying: "But those mine enemies, which would not that I should reign over them, bring hither, and slay them before me." (Luke 19:27) Or perhaps: "But whosoever shall deny me before men, him will I also deny before my Father which is in heaven. Think not that I am come to send peace on earth: I came not to send peace, but a sword." (Matt 10:33—34)

Will Mr. Maar denounce both Judaism and Christianity as "violent religions"?

Of course, Mr. Maar will retort by saying that not one Christian and not one Jew has been apprehended trying to kill Americans, and that all suspects so far have been Muslim.

But then again, perhaps Mr. Maar should recall that before September 11, the biggest terrorist threat Americans had been facing and fighting against for decades now (and probably continue to face on a daily basis) is the threat, often fulfilled with terrible criminal actions, of anti-abortion terrorists bombing abortion clinics and shooting doctors willing to perform abortions. Most such terrorists were Christians acting in the name of God, justifying their actions by reciting verses and passages (e.g., (Ps.139:13-16, Isa. 49:1,5, Jer.1:5). Such terrorism has been so successful that abortion clinics are no longer available in more than 80% of America's counties. Should Mr. Maar declare that Christianity is a violent religion, then?

Or perhaps Mr. Maar should impugn Judaism because not two weeks ago a bunch of extremist Jews acting in the name of Judaism and belonging to the extremist Jewish Defense League, a terrorist organization identified as such by the FBI, decided that it was time to give Arab and Muslim Americans "a wake up call" by bombing some mosques and the offices of Arab American Congressman Darryl Issa. Should Mr. Maar declare that Judaism is a violent religion, then?

Religions, like everything else in life, can be used for elevating humanity and they can be abused for debasing it. Islam is being abused today by a group of frustrated fanatics, just as are Christianity, Judaism, and any other religion. It is the responsibility of those who seek peace—the majority of us—to counter the irresponsible lynch calls by the likes of Mr. Maar and to announce that we will not tolerate, ever, irresponsible hate mongering, wherever it may dwell.

—January 2, 2002

Interviewing the Palestinian-Israeli conflict

I have watched literally hundreds of interviews by the US media of Israeli officials, spokespersons, scholars and journalists sympathetic to the Israeli point of
view, and yet, I can count with the fingers of one hand the number of times when
the interview was not merely a forum for the pro-Israeli guest to repeat, unchallenged in any way, meaningful or otherwise, the usual Israeli mantra that Israel is
acting out of pure self-defense, that Yasir Arafat and the Palestinians are solely
and completely responsible for the violence, and that the only way out of the crisis is a yet a stronger show of Israeli strength.

But one such rare event where the discussion unexpectedly veered off the usual
charted course took place this past Sunday on This Week with Sam Donaldson
and Cokie Roberts when the usually easy going, diffident George Stephanapolous
took the shockingly bold stand against George Will's assertion that the only language that Arafat and the Palestinians understand is the language of violence. His
response to Will consisted in making the following observation: in 1999, when
the Palestinians, for the first time in their long ordeal, had been given a bit of
hope that perhaps they were on their way of getting rid of the occupation, not a
single Israeli was killed in a terrorist act. Stephanapolous then took the next, even
bolder step of proposing that maybe what is required to bring about a lasting
peace is not more but less violence from the Israelis. What the Palestinians need,
Stephanapolous said, is more hope, not more shelling. George Will's reply was an
uncharacteristic bewildered stare and dead silence.

Only in the context of a media that has totally abandoned its mission of seeking
the truth at any cost, whenever the topic of investigation is the Palestinian-Israeli
conflict, would Stephanapolous's factual remark be described as "bold". In the
world of honest intellectual discourse, Stephanapolous's observations and proposals would be described as the most elementary manifestation of rational common
sense.

But in the real world of the US media, even such a low threshold of commonsensical honesty seems to be above what America's journalists are able to deliver or live up to.

Here are, for example, four questions that are rarely, if ever, asked by self-style tough guys of American journalism, such as Chris Matthews, Bill O'Reilly, Geraldo Riviera, or even the respectable Wolf Blitzer or Larry King:

(1) Israel has been "cracking down" on terrorism for three decades now, and yet to this day suicide bombings continue to take place—why does Israel continue following a policy that is patently a failure?

(2) If Israel were serious about a long-lasting peace with the Palestinians, then why did it double the size of its settlements in the occupied territories between 1993 and 2000?

(3) If Israel really wants Arafat to reign in militants, as it says it does, then why does it make it both politically and physically impossible for him to do so by humiliating him, denouncing him as a criminal, and physically dismantling his security apparatus and the infrastructure of his authority?

(4) If Israel were really interested in ensuring the security of its citizens, then why does it carry out assassinations, knowing full well that such assassinations will only trigger another wave of suicide bombings and escalate the cycle of violence?

Alongside their startling unwillingness to ask the tough questions, America's talk show hosts are also guilty of another host of journalistic infractions that severely undermine their mission of offering their viewers the best possible honest rendering of reality. Here are some of those infractions:

(1) Rarely interviewing a non-Palestinian/non-Arab supporter of the Palestinian cause, while often interviewing non-Israeli pro-Israel speakers, even though very qualified such scholars and activists do exist;

(2) Blatantly loading questions in favor of Israel: as in, why is Arafat letting Hamas engage in terror? or, will Sharon abandon his policy of restraint?

(3) Rarely seeking a Palestinian-American living in the Occupied Territories for interviews and reactions, while often seeking out Israeli-Americans living in Israel;

(4) Rarely, if ever, having the interview be focused on Palestinian suffering and what the Israelis need to do to stop it, but often having the interview be about the terror Israelis are suffering and what the Palestinians need to do about it;

According to a recent Arab American Discrimination Committee poll, no more than 3% of Americans are aware that the Palestinians are under occupation. This should come as no surprise, given that the most basic questions on the conflict are rarely, if ever asked, by otherwise competent and insightful journalists, and given that most elementary practices of fair interviewing are often violated when the interviewee is a supporter of the Palestinian cause.

How can the truth emerge when we don't ask the right questions and when those with the answers are muzzled unfairly?

—February 6, 2002 (The Pittsburgh Post-Dispatch)

Way beyond contempt

Take a pound of hypocrisy, add a good portion of cynicism, sprinkle generously with brazenness, then top everything off with as much hubris as your heart desires (in the style of Emeril Agassi's overdosing on garlic), and then have a stand-in chef who truly believes that such a concoction is not only a tasty meal, but more importantly, a healthy dish to be eaten in gusto, no questions asked—and there you have in a nutshell the Bush administration's style of government: government by outright bamboozlement.

The supply of examples illustrating the growing contempt from our executive for the most basic principles of transparency and the rule of law is not only embarrassingly—and alarmingly—plentiful: in fact, it continues to grow, daily, heedlessly, just as a chorus of anger and outrage is at last beginning to rise.

Here are but a few gem examples:

Vice President Dick Cheney refuses to share any information about his energy task force meetings with Enron and other energy execs. Why? Because, president Bush explained, he and his people ought to be able to freely seek and get advice from anyone they please, without the burdensome chore of having report to the American people who those advisors are or what kind of advice he may be receiving. Mr. President, how about doing it right once and for all: just fire Ari Fleicher and his inflated staff—or better yet, issue an executive order to abolish the press secretary's job, then restore it in case your successor is a Democrat) so that you and your crack men and women can concentrate, fully, one hundred percent, on the war against terror and on taking care of the people's business without having to worry about the pesky, messy task of explaining yourself. That would save you a lot time, the tax payers a lots of money, and would deprive the hopelessly biased media of any opportunities to take cheap shots at you. (Am I exaggerating? You be the judge: back in November, president bush overturned—by unilateral fiat—the 1978 presidential Records Act. Reason given: the need to re-establish an "orderly process" in sharing information. A couple more of such moves to insulate the president from accountability, and Ari Fleicher's job is out the window.)

More gems: while hundreds of Arabs and Muslims (citizens, permanent residents, student, as well as illegal aliens) were rounded up and jailed with callous disregard for their most basic civil rights, and as President Bush moved to suspend attorney client privileges for suspected (not convicted) terrorists and to set up military tribunals, a move by the FBI to establish mechanisms for obtaining more efficiently information about firearm holders was blocked by the White House. Reason: the federal government cannot, in good conscience, even if the nation is supposedly at grave peril, infringe on the right of its citizens to carry lethal weapons.

Another gem: as soon as George Bush took office, one of the first things he directed his people to do was to abandon his predecessor's efforts for a multilateral crackdown on the very types of overseas tax havens that have allowed Enron to engage in its mind-boggling shenanigans. Reason given, as Treasury Secretary Paul O'Neil put it: the Administration will not "interfere with the internal tax policy decisions of sovereign nations".

And speaking of sovereignty and non-interference: as Argentina teeters on the edge of total economic and social collapse (the political collapse has already taken place), President Bush still manages to argue, without a hint of embarrassment, that nations going through economic hard times must first "make themselves more attractive to foreign investors"—a code phrase for the very IMF policies that have wrecked havoc in Argentina and much of the Third World—before the industrialized world should come to their rescue. And to prove that he was not just mouthing bromides, the President directed his administration to torpedo European efforts to double their development aid to countries in crisis. And this took place the very day before the president's State of the Union, where he enunciated America's long-haul commitment to rebuilding Afghanistan and paying more attention to trouble spots around the world before they careen out of control.

More: asked why journalists are not allowed nearer than a few hundred feet to the Al-Qaeda "detainees" at Guantanamo base, and why they are not being allowed to photograph their faces, Defense Secretary explained that doing so would violate the rights of the "detainees" under the Geneva Conventions. This is the very same Donald Rumsfeld who has not tired of telling us that the "detainees" are not prisoners of war, that they are not entitled to protections under the Geneva

Conventions, and that the United States has every right to treat them as it damn pleases.

But here is my favorite: asked about what, if anything, was planned in anticipation of the smoldering heat at Guantanamo come summertime, Donald Rumsfels explained, not missing a beat: "To be in an eight-by-eight cell in beautiful, sunny Guantanamo Bay, Cuba, is not a—inhumane treatment. And it has a roof."

The level of bald faced, shameless duplicity of president Bush and his men, their brazen flouting of international law, their "we-will-do-as-we-please" approach to government, is outpaced only by the extent to which they have gone out of their way to insult the intelligence of the American people. The American people may, sadly enough, tolerate many evils, but they will not for long accept a president that does worse than deceive them behind their backs: he lies and deceives them straight to their faces.

—February 8, 2002

From silence to the bullet

The day will come, hopefully soon, when everyone, and not just those watching the Palestinian-Israeli conflict up close, will look back to this time with utter astonishment and disbelief and ask: Why was the American media totally silent over Israeli war crimes against Palestinian children? Why didn't they rise up, through their editorials and their on-air commentaries, with disgust and indignation over Israel's policy of killing children and innocent civilians as a tactic to pressure Palestinians to turn against their leadership?

When such a day comes, will editors be able to legitimately plead ignorance? Unlikely. The evidence has been overwhelming, and everywhere: from day one of this Intifada, Amnesty International, Human Rights Watch, Peace Now, Gush Shalom, B'tselem, along with the United Nations Human Rights Commission, and many, many other groups, have been denouncing the Israeli army's policy of shooting at children to kill.

As far back as December 2000, only three months after the outbreak of the Intifada, Amnesty International concluded that: "For a force trained in policing riots and equipped and prepared for stone throwers, neither stones nor petrol bombs should be lethal. Therefore there should be no need for the use of firearms, let alone lethal force, against stone throwers."

And yet, the killing and maiming has continued, unabated, to the tune of 80 Palestinian children younger than 15 and 197 below the age of 18, and tens of thousands of wounded, while the media have stood by in utter silence. Indeed, not one editorial in any of the main media outlets that I can remember since the outbreak of the Intifada a year and a half ago has been published that stated, unambiguously or otherwise, that although Israel has a right to defend itself, it has no right to kill and maim children and innocent civilians as a pressure tactic; as a policy. Keeping to a long-standing tradition of ignoring what human rights organizations have to say (unless they are targeting America's official "enemies"), the US mainstream media have decided to simply look the other way.

But then reports of such atrocities began to appear in the mainstream media itself, under the very noses of editorial writers. Last October, for instance, in a gripping article by New York Times reporter Chris Hedges, published in the October issue of Harper's magazine, we read about the Israeli army's routine practice of inciting Palestinian children and then shooting them to kill. Hedges also appeared on NPR's Fresh Air on Oct. 30, 2001, where he told millions of listeners the following: "I've seen death squads kill families in Algeria or El Salvador. But I'd never seen soldiers bait or taunt kids like this and then shoot them for sport. It was—I just—even now, I find it almost inconceivable. And I went back every day, and every day it was the same."

Then came the eyewitness accounts of Israeli soldiers who are now refusing to serve in the occupied territories, citing their objection to "illegal orders" for unleashing death and violence against civilians. In their statements, the soldiers state: "We, combat officers and soldiers who have served the state of Israel for long weeks every year…were issued commands and directives that had nothing to do with the security of our country, and that had the sole purpose of perpetuating our control over the Palestinian people; we, whose eyes have seen the bloody toll this occupation exacts from both sides; we shall not continue to fight beyond the 1967 borders in order to dominate, expel, starve and humiliate an entire people."

And lately, a heated, passionate debate within Israel itself is raging about Israel's crimes against civilians. In a Feb. 10 piece in Israel's Ha'aretz newspaper, veteran journalist Gideon Levy wrote bitterly that "the Israeli army has totally shaken off any and all moral responsibility for the killing of these children", noting that "in not one of these cases did the Israeli army spokesman take the trouble to do the minimum human necessary thing—to express sorrow at the death of the children. The only conclusion is that the Israeli army is not sorry about their killing. That is the message to those who did the killing and to the families of those who were killed. No less grave, the Israeli army did not even contemplate investigating the circumstances of the deaths".

Levy goes on to observe: "The fact is that not everything is permitted. When the Israeli army wanted to prevent immoral and illegal actions, it was able to do so. There are two offences that Israeli army soldiers have rarely committed during the years of the occupation—sexual harassment and looting."

As is well known, Israel cannot engage in any atrocities if the government of the United States decides that it must stop. And the US government will not tolerate such atrocities if a chorus of outrage were raised by the US media. If the New York Times, the Washington Post, the Philadelphia Inquirer, the Wall Street Journal, the USA Today, the LA Times, and other papers, along with commentators on NPR, CNN, MSNBC and other media outlets, started publishing and airing unambiguous condemnations of Israel's policy of killing children, you can bet that the US administration will ensure that such killing stops at once before the outcry against Israel spirals out of control—and anything spiraling out of control is the thing the US (and any government) fears the most. (A campaign of outcries against US moves to do as they please with the Taleban and Al Qaeda "detainees", with total disregard to the Geneva Conventions, certainly has pressured the administration to begin worrying at least about seeming to respect international law.)

In other words, the moral responsibility of the US media is clear and direct: the chain from silence to bullet is present, real, indisputable and straightforward, and no matter how they choose to justify this silence, members of the US media cannot shirk that responsibility and maintain any claim to moral integrity.

Members of the US media need to take a clear stand against the illegal practices of the Israeli army now, before the train of history passes them and the ignominy of having stood silent while crimes against humanity were committed forever blots their already soiled record on this unending tragedy; a tragedy in whose prolonged agony they must sadly accept a share of responsibility.

—February 21, 2002 (The Jordan Times)

How to influence the US media

To those who insist that American journalists are by and large well-meaning, that they do not deceive, mislead, or lie, that they are open to reason and persuasion, that they have the good of their profession at heart, that they are moral, conscientious, and above all fair, I propose that they take the following into their reckoning.

On March 17, 2002, Nolan Finley, editorial page editor of The Detroit News, published an op-ed piece in which he wrote, "The ugly little secret of the Middle East conflict is that a favorite target of Palestinian terrorists are the children, teenagers and young adults of Israel." In that piece, Mr. Finley cites no reports, no findings or investigations, no official statements, showing that indeed Palestinians "appear to be intentionally killing Israel's kids." And yet, he had no qualms titling his piece "Israel's children are the target of Middle East terror campaign". By contrast, extensive studies and reports by Amnesty International, Human Rights Watch, Bet'slem, and other organizations, along with credible eyewitness accounts, such as those of New York Times journalist Christopher Hedges, have established beyond the shadow of doubt that the IDF routinely and systematically targets and kills Palestinian children. (In fact, I myself published an op-ed on December 9, 2001, on the very pages that Mr. Finley edits, quoting and describing such a piece by Mr. Hedges). And yet, not one word of indignation or outrage from Mr. Finley, or any editor that I can recall, has ever been sounded or written bout the well-documented intentional killing by the IDF of Palestinian children.

March 15, 2002: I email the ombudsman of one of the largest circulation papers in the US east coast, complaining about their front-page picture that day showing Palestinians dragging the body of an alleged Palestinian informant. The complaint comes on the heels of a long campaign by myself and other local activists for at least an occasional front-page picture of Palestinian suffering (in the 18 months of the Intifada, the face of a Palestinian victim was shown twice on their front page!). "And you don't want me to be angry?" I title my email, and then go on in the body to write: "We plead and plead with you for a front page photo of Palestinian suffering, and what do you serve us in return: a bestialisation of the Palestinians." The ombudsman fires back within minutes with the following: "I think today's front page photo accurately portrayed the horror of what happened in Manger Square. When the awful day comes that Palestinian suffering captures the main headline of the day, then I suspect that will be the main photo, too." I am stunned and write back: "I didn't realize that headlines were captured by events directly, with no interference from papers or editors!"

March 9, 2002: I attend the annual National Arab American Journalists Association (NAAJA) gathering in Chicago, where I get a chance to meet reporters and editors from the Chicago press. In one particular panel, I get into a heated exchange with two editors from the Chicago Tribune. The bone of contention is the word "occupied" and I complain about the frequent use of the word "disputed" instead. "But there is a dispute," one the editors insists, to my astonishment, "and so we can say that the territories are 'disputed'." "But 'disputed' connotes that it remains to be determined who owns what," I retort, upset more than angry over having to have this conversation. "Why not use a perfectly well-defined, legally established, and universally accepted term, rather than pick a term that is misleading and morally suspect?" One of the editors sententiously points out the infamous discrepancy between the French and the English versions of the UN resolution referring to "les territories" vs "territories", and concludes that "a case can, and has been mounted, by the other side, and so it is our duty to remain detached and simply point that the territories are disputed." Little effect did the argument that the very same resolution he cited declares in no uncertain terms that no territories are to be legitimately acquired by force.

Rewind to one year ago: February 28, 2001, only a few days to Ariel Sharon's ascension to the Prime Ministership. I submit a compelling op-ed piece from Hanan Ashrawi to the Commentary Page editor of a large circulation east coast US paper. I had queried the editor a week earlier about the possibility of publishing a piece from Dr. Ashrawi, and he had responded enthusiastically. But a day after I submit the piece, the editor writes back the following: "my editors objected, pointing out (rightly) that the piece is strident, calls names, is inaccurate (for example, I know of no case so far in which Sharon has pursued war, so the phrase 'warmongering present' is simply not factual, unless one is using it in a partisan fashion, in which case the word becomes meaningless, or at the very best, inaccessible to my readers), and very redundant."

Facing such absurdities, should activists trying to nudge the US media to cover the Palestinian-Israeli conflict accurately and professionally simply throw their arms up?

The answer was vividly provided me in another exchange I had with a Chicago Tribune editor back at the NAAJA conference. In a panel on the mainstream media, the editor in question patiently lectured us about the need to examine coverage "over a period of time" and to avoid nitpicking. I raised my hand and informed the editor that we, at Palestine Media Watch, routinely publish detailed reports that examine coverage "over a period of time," and that we have discovered for instance, among other things, that out of all the front page photographs on the Palestinian-Israeli conflict, more than 90% of them depict Israeli suffering, with the remaining 10% consisting of your charred cars and bombed building. Given that the death toll on the Palestinian side is four to five times that of Israeli side, and given that more than 200 of the killed are children, I asked, was that not a flagrant example of bias? The editor grunted and waved his hand dismissively. I pressed for an explanation, and he answered: "I can only tell you that the other side complains much more about our coverage than your side". "Is that an explanation, or a justification, or an excuse?" I shouted back. He merely repeated his assertion and moved on to the next question.

In other words, after all is said and done, after all the high talk about journalistic integrity and a commitment to rendering a faithful image of reality, it all boils down to who complains the loudest, who is the biggest nuisance, and who makes the most trouble. A sorry state for an institution that prides itself (and loudly) for being a model for the rest of the world, but if that's the deal on the table, then we have only ourselves to blame if we don't turn into relentless irate nags who won't rest no matter what.

—March 26, 2002 (Address to the Institute on Religion and Democracy)

Framing the struggle

One of the tragedies of the Palestinian-Israeli struggle is the reality that Palestinians have suffered and continue to suffer such an array of injustices that just advertising them to the world, let alone fighting and resisting them, can consume one emotionally, intellectually and physically beyond the point of exhaustion.

As a result, the bottom line of what Palestinians want is somehow lost in the torrent of outcries raised against the unending stream of Israeli transgressions. At least here in the United States, if one were to ask a relatively well-informed, well-educated American, "What do Palestinians want?", chances are that one would not get a clear and straightforward answer. For the above-average American, the Palestinian-Israeli conflict is perceived to be complex beyond comprehension, beyond hope, so that Palestinian outcries, even when they are received favorably (and many of them are), somehow do not leave the residue of sympathy they should be leaving.

One of the reasons why this is the case is that Palestinian grievances have not been properly framed within the context of a clear and easy to understand moral and political goal. Demands to "end the occupation," "abide by U.N. resolutions," "dismantle settlements," "grant Palestinians a viable state," "ensure territorial integrity," "stop the humiliation of Palestinian civilians," to list only a few of a long list of legitimate demands, all point to necessary steps that must be taken to reach a lasting solution, but fail to provide the constructive framing within which the Palestinian quest for freedom can be articulated. They fail to articulate a simple slogan of what Palestinians want.

Compare this with the carefully crafted and carefully managed framing from the Israeli side: the No. 1 concern for Israel, we are told over and over again, is Israel's "security." The whole history of the conflict, along with the rationale behind Israeli actions, are reduced to one single word: "security."

With this framework in place, the job of explaining actions and reactions can be carried out in a coherent, consistent manner, thus creating the illusion of truth.

Why has Israel re-invaded the West Bank? To restore security. Why does Israel cut off whole towns? To deter "terrorism." Why did Israel invade the West Bank and Gaza along with the Sinai and the Golan Heights in 1967? Because it wanted to create a "security buffer zone." Why did Israel invade Lebanon in 1982? To pursue "terrorists" who were jeopardizing Israel's "security." Why does Israel build settlements deep in Palestinian territory? To ensure "security."

To say the least, the strategy has been effective.

Indeed, one of the oldest tricks that good propaganda machines know how to turn is the trick of coherence. A tightly coherent picture compels one to believe that it is based on reality, even when it is based on pure myths and falsifications. By the same token, a fragmented story, even when based on glaring reality, is hard to absorb; its reality is reduced to disconnected anecdotes, each eliciting sympathy, but together creating a world of confusion.

Fragmentation of the Palestinian message, of course, is not only precisely what the Israeli occupation wants: it is something that the occupation has consciously promoted on all fronts: politically, economically, socially and militarily. Scatter the opposition and buy time. And with time, the fragments will grow smaller and eventually will vanish. (It worked quite nicely in the United States with the Native Americans—Israel is doing nothing but emulating its benevolent guardian.)

On their part, therefore, Palestinians and their supporters should announce a clear and simple message that can be repeated over and over again so that when you ask anyone, no matter how distantly they may be following the conflict, "What do Palestinians want?" they will readily answer, "They want an independent state."

Asking for a fully independent state is a moral goal that no fair-minded person could reject on its own merits: it is an internationally recognized right, and one that anyone, including Americans, can immediately grasp and identify with. And it is also a politically measurable desideratum: full independence means total evacuation of the occupying force from Palestinian land.

If the world were to clearly grasp the one goal that Palestinians want—full independence—then Palestinian actions could begin to be framed as actions towards a specific goal, and not just as manifestations of anger, of frustration, of desperation, of hatred—the framing that the occupation wants the world to maintain about the Palestinian struggle. Within this framing, talk of "terrorism" can at long last be properly contextualized, both historically and politically.

After all, didn't Jews engage in terrorism against civilians when they fought for the establishment of their state? And politically, making "independence" the primary issue in the conflict, rather than the looser goal of "security," can reverse the cause-effect relationship: "security" will ensue from "independence," as it has always in all conflicts pitting an occupied people against its occupier, rather "independence" from "security."

Palestinians should begin to push one clear message and rally around that one message, so that the whole world can answer with one simple word the question "what do Palestinians want?" And that word should be: "independence."

—April 21, 2002 (The Jordan Times)

Not bias, but mediocrity

A word I no longer use when I complain to reporters, editors, and editorial boards, about their coverage of the Palestinian-Israeli conflict is the word "bias".

Accusations of media "bias" against Palestinians or against Israelis have become so widespread and have been bandied out for so long that they have become virtually meaningless. Instead, now I use the word "mediocrity". I accuse the media not of intentionally slanting the news to favor the Israeli narrative, or of consciously highlighting Israeli suffering at the expense of Palestinian suffering, but of practicing "shabby journalism".

And what do I mean with "shabby journalism"?

It is a mark of shabby journalism, for instance, to use the word "retaliation" without quotes, time and again, sometimes in headlines, to characterize Israeli actions, as if a reporter could ever divine the intentions of those who order strikes against Palestinians.[5] How would a reporter know that an action is a "retaliation" and not an act of "provocation" or an act of "collective punishment"? Moreover, why is the word "retaliation" never used to characterize the actions of Palestinians, even when the perpetrators openly declare that the actions were in "retaliation" to specific Israeli actions?

If indeed the conflict is caught in a "cycle of violence", as we are told time and again, then why are Israelis always portrayed as reacting and Palestinians always as initiating?

Another mark of shabby journalism is the adoption, often without surrounding quotes, of euphemisms put forward by spokesmen of the Israeli Defense Forces (IDF), such as "targeted killing", "crossfire", "errant shells and bullets", to name just the most notorious.[6]

How targeted is a killing that kills its "target" (and what is "target", anyway?), but also half a dozen civilians along the way (often women and children)? Why is it that only Palestinians are killed in a "crossfire", never an Israeli? And why are Israelis always making a "regrettable mistake", even when the "mistake" is a perfectly predictable consequence of a callous spraying of bullets or indiscriminate firing of shells in a thickly populated civilian area?

More notorious still is usage of the word "terror" exclusively to describe Palestinian acts of violence, but never to describe Israeli acts of violence, even when the acts are those of Jewish settlers run amuck, killing Palestinian civilians (and sometimes children) precisely to terrorize Palestinian populations. Instead, the word "vigilante" is used, conveying to the impression that the perpetrator of the terrorist action is merely taking the law into his own hands, perhaps out of frustration with "the policy of restraint"—yet another euphemism—practiced by the IDF.[7]

More serious than subtle, and not so subtle, euphemisms, is reporting that outright misleads the reader. A striking example of this is the repeated use of the figure 95% to characterize the "offers" (yet another euphemism—one "offers" presents, not land that one does not own) allegedly made by Ehud Barak at Camp David. To begin with, the figure 95% itself has been sharply disputed (the latest revelations put the figure around 70%).[8] But worse than the figure is the total absence of any maps depicting the "offers".

The Palestinians did not object to the figure 95% (or any figure) as such, but to the nature of the land "offered" them: three disconnected patches of land, with settlements within Palestinian territory, with all borders tightly controlled by Israel, with little water rights, with virtually no sovereign control over the token patchworks of Jerusalem proposed, to name just the most important objections. How can readers grasp the nature of Palestinian objections without maps? And what other conclusion will they come to when they hear that the Palestinians rejected a deal that offered them 95% of what they wanted, other than the conclusion that Israel wishes us to draw: that the Palestinians are not serious about settling peacefully?[9]

An equally egregious mark of shabby journalism is a prevailing self-imposed self-censorship that dismisses any story that seriously challenges the prevailing narrative openly adopted by all the major media outlets (if their editorials are any indication of that narrative). According to that narrative, Israel is fighting to ensure its security; at times it unfortunately uses excessive force; at times it pursues unwise policies (e.g., settlements); but over all, Israel is a democracy, it is respectful of the rule of law, and it is mindful of human rights concerns. Hence, when a story is published about Israeli soldiers routinely inciting, taunting and baiting, Palestinian children to throw stones at them, only to shoot (and kill) them "for sport", as veteran New York Times reporter Chris Hedges wrote in a piece he published in the October 2001 issue of Harper's Magazine[10] (and repeated in his October 31 appearance on NPR's Fresh Air[11]), the scandalous revelation is treated as an anomaly, an exception, to be shelved, rather than picked up and front-paged and headlined, as the killing of Israeli children is.

So, is the media "biased" against Palestinians? The question itself is a bad question, because it lets the media off the hook much too easily. Indeed, that is precisely why reporters and editors love to be accused of "bias", since they have a ready-made answer: "if we are being criticized from both sides," they cheerfully answer, "then we must be doing our job."

But the fact is that the media is not doing its job. Coverage of the Palestinian-Israeli conflict is marred by clear marks of sloppy journalism: loaded euphemisms and unreflective language, double standards, incomplete and outright misleading reporting, and unhealthy self-censorship. The media may very well not be "biased", but is certainly is mediocre when it comes to covering the Palestinian-Israeli conflict.

—May 29, 2002 (The Jordan Times)

Harsh words trample Palestinians' hopes

What should Palestinians think when they read, as reported on May 7, 2002, by Israel's most respected paper, Yedioth Ahronoth, that Israeli school children, some of them teenagers only a few years away from joining military service, send letters in which they write "please kill a lot of Arabs", "I pray for you that you return home safely, and kill at least ten for me," "Let the Palestinians, may God blacken their name, burn in Hell. Punch holes in them with your M-16 and bomb them"?[12]

What should they think when they read that the spiritual leader of a key party in the current Israeli coalition government has publicly used, more than once, such hate speech as, "May the Holy Name visit retribution on the Arabs' heads, and cause their seed to be lost, and annihilate them, and cause them to be vanquished and cause them to be cast from the world. It is forbidden to be merciful to them, you must give them missiles, with relish—annihilate them. Evil ones, damnable ones"?[13]

What should they think when one of the most respected American journalists, New York Time reporter Chris Hedges, publishes a story in which he states that he has watched Israeli soldiers day after day taunt Palestinian children and then "shoot them for sport" (his own words), and yet no one in the media, let alone the US administration, expresses outrage and indignation over the practice?[14]

What should they think when the Majority Leader of the United States Congress Advocates, on national television and on the record, the transfer of Palestinian populations from the Occupied Territories—a practice officially designated as a war crime by the Fourth Geneva Conventions? "I'm content to have Israel grab the entire West Bank"? Mr. Armey said, pointing out that "[t]here are many Arab nations that have many hundreds of thousands of acres of land.[15]

What should they think when they read one of America's most respected lawyers and self-proclaimed civil and human rights defender, Harvard Professor Alan Dershowitz, propose—with perfect matter-of-fact moral confidence—an outright war crime: "for every attack, Israel should after giving the residents 24 hours to leave, bulldoze a Palestinian village that has been "used as a base for terrorist operations."?[16] Also, how should they think that Professor Dershowitz's remarks have elicited little more than a yawn from his colleagues, the legal establishment, and the media in general?

What should they think when they hear tens of thousands of Jewish-American supporters of Israel loudly boo and hiss one of the top officials in the US government, deputy defense secretary, Paul Wolfowitz (himself a long time hawkish supporter of Israel) for simply suggesting that innocent Palestinians hurt in the current conflict deserve also some sympathy"?[17]

What should they think when they read that America's top law enforcement official, Attorney General John Ashcroft, believes that while "Christianity is a faith in which God sends his son to die for you", "Islam is a religion in which God requires you to send your son to die for him"?[18]

What should they think when they hear that Israel's most "dovish" Prime minister, Ehud Barak, believes that the Palestinians are the product of a culture "in which to tell a lie…creates no dissonance. They don't suffer from the problem of telling lies that exists in Judaeo-Christian culture. Truth is seen as an irrelevant category. There is only that which serves your purpose and that which doesn't."[19]

What should they think when they read that the platform of the political party in power in Israel, Ariel Sharon's Likud, still retains language that asserts that there should be "No Palestinian state west of the Jordan river"?

And what should they think when they read that in spite of such unyielding rejectionism, the President of the United States still openly declares that "Ariel Sharon" is "a man of peace"—Ariel Sharon, the very same man responsible for what Amnesty International and Human Rights watch have called the "war crimes of Jenin"[20], and the very man found by an Israeli court personally responsible for the massacre of more than 800 Palestinian civilians in the refugee camps of Sabra and Shatilla?[21]

Should they think that Israel truly means to co-exist with them, or should they suspect that it aims to conquer them? And should they truly believe that America is an honest broker, or should they suspect that America is fully on the side of one party, even while claiming impartiality?

—June 17, 2002 (The Baltimore Sun)

Next time, remind them

Next time you hear someone argue that Israel has no colonial designs over the West Bank, Gaza, and Jerusalem, remind them of the following facts: In 1972, the total settlement population in Gaza and the West Bank was 1,500; today it is over 210,000. In 1972, total settler population in East Jerusalem was 6,900; today it is above 170,400 and between 1993 and 2000, the total settler population in the Occupied Territories doubled.[22]

Next time you hear someone claim that UN resolution 242 is ambiguous about how much of the territories Israel invaded in 1967 it must cede, remind them that the resolution's opening sentence asserts "the inadmissibility of the acquisition of territory by war."[23] Also, remind them that UN Resolution 465 "determines that all measures taken by Israel to change the physical character, demographic composition, institutional structure of status of the Palestinian and other Arab territories occupied since 1967, including Jerusalem, or any part thereof, have no legal validity and that Israel's policy and practices of settling parts of its population and new Immigrants in those territories constitute a flagrant violation of the fourth Geneva convention relative to the protection of civilian persons in time of war and also constitute a serious obstruction to achieving a comprehensive, just and lasting peace in the Middle East."[24]

Next time you hear someone argue that Ariel Sharon is a man of peace, that deep down he does seek a solution that will guarantee the right and respect the dignity of all parties, remind them of the following from President Jimmy Carter—not a stranger to peace-making: "[Ariel Sharon's] rejection of all peace agreements that included Israeli withdrawal from Arab lands, his invasion of Lebanon, his provocative visit to the Temple Mount, the destruction of villages and homes, the arrests of thousands of Palestinians and his open defiance of President George W. Bush's demand that he comply with international law have all been orchestrated to accomplish his ultimate goals: to establish Israeli settlements as widely as possible throughout occupied territories and to deny Palestinians a cohesive political existence."[25]

Next time you hear someone say that the Palestinian Authority deliberately launched the Second Intifada in reaction to the failure of Camp David II, remind them of the following conclusion from the Mitchell Report: "...we have no basis on which to conclude that there was a deliberate plan by the PA to initiate a campaign of violence at the first opportunity".[26]

Next time you hear someone claim that Palestinian textbooks incite Palestinian children to hated for Jews and violence, remind them of what professor Nathan Brown of the George Washington University wrote in a study he published in October 2001: "the Palestinian curriculum is not a war curriculum; while highly nationalistic, it does not incite hatred, violence, and anti-Semitism."[27]

Next time you hear someone claim that unlike suicide bombers, the Israeli army never intentionally targets civilians, remind them of what New York Times reporter Chris Hedges said on NPR's Fresh Air on October 30, 2001, about the Israeli Defense forces: "I've seen kids shot in Sarajevo.... I've seen death squads kill families in Algeria or El Salvador. But I'd never seen soldiers bait or taunt kids like this and then shoot them for sport."[28]

Next time you hear someone claim that the Palestinians were never negotiating in good faith in Camp David and later, that they had never meant to take seriously any proposals put forward to them, remind them of the join-statement issued after the Taba talks in Egypt, in late January, 2001—a statement that Ehud Barak officially endorsed: "the two sides declare that they have never been closer to reaching an agreement and it is thus our shared belief that the remaining gaps could be bridged with the resumption of negotiations following the Israeli elections."[29]

Next time you hear someone claim that 98 percent of the Palestinians in the West Bank and Gaza are under Palestinian rule, remind them of what Israeli human rights group Btselem concluded recently: "research reveals that while the built-up areas of the settlements constitute only 1.7% of the land in the West Bank, the municipal boundaries are over three times as large: 6.8%. Regional councils constitute an additional 35.1%. Thus, a total of 41.9% of the area in the West Bank is controlled by the settlements."[30]

And next time you hear someone say the whole Arab world must stretch hand forward and offer a comprehensive peace to Israel, and that until then Israel is justified in remaining suspicious of Palestinian intentions, remind them that the

Arabs did precisely that in Beirut, on March 28, 2002, when they issued an official statement that read in part: "the Arab countries affirm the following: a. Consider the Arab-Israeli conflict ended, and enter into a peace agreement with Israel, and provide security for all the states of the region. b. Establish normal relations with Israel in the context of this comprehensive peace."[31]

Remind them of how Ariel Sharon reacted to that initiative: with a full scale attack on Palestinian towns and refugee camps in the West Bank, beginning on March 29, 2002, and by perpetrating what the Red Cross, Amnesty International and Human Rights Watch have called "the war crimes of Jenin".[32]

—June 24, 2002

The one-way forward

Not that we have had one good week since the second Intifada started in September 2000, but this was a particularly bad and ugly week for those who struggle for justice and peace in the Middle East: President George Bush gave a speech that could just as well have been written by a Likud speech writer; Congressman Earl Hilliard of Alabama was defeated by AIPAC money; Ariel Sharon's Belgium trials were thrown out over a technicality; and CNN spectacularly buckled under mighty pro-Israeli pressures. And so we must ask: What should the lesson be for us, Arabs, Muslims and those who support the Palestinians' quest for independence? What should we learn from the setbacks of this nasty week?

When Ariel Sharon began his military reinvasion of the West Bank in March, his intent was to fully destroy the nascent Palestinian state's infrastructure and to set the stage for a full reoccupation of the West Bank. And he did manage to do that to a certain extent, but he was reined back and had to pace his murderous assault. Why? Because ordinary Arab citizens around the world mobilized en masse. It was not governments who kept Sharon in check, not any threat to stop the flow of oil (there was none issued, except for Saddam Hussein's half-hearted gesture), not any threat to halt cooperation in the "war against terrorism", but the threat of a popular revolt that could spiral out of control.

We need to keep that lesson well in mind in these difficult times, when we ask ourselves what can be done to get us out of this absurd situation. Justice is on our side, the vast majority of the world is on our side, so why do the Israelis continue to score points while we keep on falling behind? What can we do, besides lamenting our fate, to make the headway we should be making?

Looking back closer to ourselves here in the US, the answer is simple: pro-Israel Jews and their supporters are constantly on the move, are constantly mobilized, are highly motivated and organized, and wage their battle to promote what they believe in every single day.

When Hilliard was picked as the political season's victim of the year by AIPAC, pro-Israel supporters did not whine, wince and wring hands: they sent checks, spread the word, and kept at it until he was defeated. They mobilized their well-oiled machine and got things done.

In sharp contrast, what did Arab and Muslim Americans do to support Hilliard? I had a chat with an AP reporter from Alabama last week, a few days to the run-off, and he complained that aside our little couple of pages that we at Palestine Media Watch had put up, he could not find anything else up by way of open support and organization for Hilliard from Arab Americans. To be sure, there was some behind-the-scene support from Arab American organizations, but nowhere nearly as much noise and publicity as the campaign should have been given by our side. Worse, Hilliard's opponent, Artur Davis, was showered with money from pro-Israel supporters, while Hilliard received relatively much less from Arab Americans.

Sure, one may argue that we are not as affluent as the pro-Israel forces—but then again, what does it take to raise a million dollars (and a million dollars would have made a huge difference)? One thousand $1,000 checks? Ten thousand $100 checks? We, Arabs and Muslims, count more than 6 million; can't we, together, come up with a million dollars to make the point that we can stop the mighty AIPAC machine?

Imagine if Hilliard had been saved by Arab/Muslim money and support? Imagine how much more encouraged those congressmen who do want to stand for what is right and good without risking political suicide would be? No, instead we sat and watched as Hilliard, an incumbent, was felled and replaced by someone who now wholly owes his election to the pro-Israel lobby. And so now the Congress is sure to get even more hysterical about not daring to criticize Israel.

But let's turn to what we can do from here on.

Last week, Ted Turner dared to suggest that Israel is also engaged in terrorism (by the way, 40 per cent of the American people do agree with him on that), and so a maelstrom followed and CNN was not only forced to rebuff and rebuke Turner, but immediately launched a 5-part series on Israeli victims, and a website that listed every single Israeli victim of suicide bombings.

What are we going to do about this? Are we going to, once again, sit idle, maybe at best protest for a few days, and then move on with our busy lives, or are we going to get obsessed with the cause and push as hard as we can—each one of us—until we get what we want: a 5-part series from CNN and a website listing each and every single child, woman and elderly Palestinian victim killed by Israel?

The Palestinian issue, and the issue of the Middle East in general, are not mere foreign policy side issues that have little effect on our lives here in the US. On the contrary, they affect us immensely—and they will continue to affect us as long as the Middle East conflict is not solved, once and for all. As long as the AIPAC lobby has the influence it has on the US policy towards the Middle East, we Arabs and Muslims will suffer the consequences (as will Americans in general, in fact, in terms of a reckless and unwise foreign policy, and in terms of an erosion of basic civil rights and due process).

We will hear absurd things like US Attorney General John Ashcroft's comment on Islam being a religion of suicide bombers, we will be characterized as a people who produces terrorists, we will be viewed as coming from a culture of weakness, divisiveness, impotence, we will be viewed the way AIPAC wants us to be viewed, to make sure that the Palestinians' plight is never fully humanized.

And that is why—in addition to our obligation to stand and defend justice and freedom for our Palestinian sisters and brothers—we need to fight every single day, must organize, constantly, must be creative and energetic, must try, and fail, and fail again, and try and try again, to get coalitions going, get people motivated, speak out, write, call, fax, distribute, volunteer, day in and day out. Our struggle is not just for an ideal: it is a crucial struggle for our own well-being and the well-being of the society we live in here and now and for the future.

Things can only get better, but only if we will ourselves to act.

—July 2, 2002 (The Jordan Times)

Imperiling democracy

And so we lost another one. Georgia's Cynthia McKinney went down, just like Earl Hilliard of Alabama before her, because the pro-Israel AIPAC lobby decided that it must be so. And so it was. Millions of dollars were mobilized by the "Israel-right-or-wrong" crowd, and as the axiom of American politics dictates, the ones with the fattest coffers won.

And now we have two more Congressmen who owe not only their election but their political career wholly to a lobby dedicated to promoting first and foremost, and above all else, the interests of a foreign government.

Is this healthy for the American political system?

Is it healthy that a local Congressional primary be decided by the priorities of a foreign lobby? Is it healthy that money would come pouring in from places that never heard of the 4th Georgia Congressional district or the 7th Alabama Congressional district, let alone be familiar with the issues that are of importance to those districts or which candidates stands for what? Are McKinney's and Hilliard's challengers truly the better choices for Georgia and Alabama?

By all considerations, both campaigns delved very little into the issues that really mattered to those voting—education, health care, jobs, the environment, public safety, crime—since both sides in both races by and large agreed very closely on what was best for their district. Instead, as always happens when little differences over substance exist, the campaigns disintegrated into mud slinging and image bashing. Could the challengers, with very little new to offer by way of ideas and solution, and no legislative experience to speak of, have been able to mount on their own the campaigns they managed to mount without the massive infusions of money and help from across the country?

Moreover, McKinney and Hilliard were two voices among a tiny minority in Congress that stood up and dared to courageously question the rubber-stamping role that Congress has come to play, and with relish and much enthusiasm, when it comes to policies regarding Israel and the Middle East. Neither McKinney nor Hilliard could be considered anti-Israel by anyone willing to pass honest and fair judgment on their voting record. They have both repeatedly voted in support of Israel, have reiterated their commitment to the "special relationship" between the United States and Israel, and have by and large towed the mainstream line. But that was not good enough for the "Israel-right-or-wrong" crowd. Both McKinney and Hilliard dared to demur on a couple of occasions, dared to ask "why?", questioned the wisdom of putting the interests of a foreign government over the interest of America, and worse of all, treated Arab and Muslim Americans as fellow citizens, entitled to have someone speak up for them and defend their most basic civil rights. And that, sadly, placed them at the fringe of American politics. They dared to dissent, and so they had to go.

And now the message has gone across loud and clear: dissent, any dissent, when it comes to American policy in the Middle East, is not only bad for your political health but could kill you. Add to that the following bonus lesson: unless you want the kiss of political death, stay clear of any Arabs or Muslims.

Many people are bitter and angry not only at what AIPAC has done in these two races, but at the devastation it has wrought on the political landscape in the past twenty years or so. They could not make do with more than 95% of the Congress flatly prostrated in the service of Israel, a foreign country, with its own priorities and its own interests, many people are thinking; they had to have 100%—they had to stifle the faintest whispers of debate and thereby kill the very lifeblood of real democracy.

And so we ask why? Why does AIPAC have a zero tolerance policy on dissent regarding Israel? Why does it make it its business that a Congresswoman from Georgia and a Congressman from Alabama be defeated for voting 90% rather than 100% in favor of Israel?

The answer is one word: fear.

Like any authoritarian power standing on a weak foundation of support, AIPAC is paranoid over the prospect that once a real debate on the Middle East is sparked, the whole magnificent edifice would crumble like a house of cards.

And it shall, in due time. How do I know?

Three weeks ago, I attended a fund-raising for Cynthia McKinney. The fundraising was not organized by a Palestinian group, or an Arab group, or a Muslim group. It was organized by a Jewish group that opposes the Israeli occupation. The people who attended the fundraising spanned the whole spectrum of races, religions, and political affiliations. As the hostess of the fundraising put it to Congresswoman McKinney when she called in to speak to the more than 100 folks in attendance: "You should see what this room looks like! There are all kinds of people here. Women in headscarves, Black and white people, Jews, Christians, and Muslims, secular humanists, old and young!" But for all their differences, the people in that room had this in common: they were against the Israeli occupation, for a just and lasting peace and co-existence in the Middle East, against religious intolerance and bigotry, whether against Jews, Christians, or Muslims, for civil rights, and against the war mongering fever that has swept across the halls of our government.

AIPAC can go on snuffing lone voices as it pleases, but with each fallen victim those who cherish America's political sovereignty and its democratic principles will only redouble their commitment and strengthen their resolve to fight for their right to elect officials who have the courage to stand up and say no to policies that are so obviously putting their whole nation in harm's way.

—August 23, 2002 (The Atlanta Journal Constitution)

Receptive Americans offer opportunity for change

For better or for worse, the US mainstream media is the principal means through which American public opinion about the Palestinian-Israeli conflict is shaped. Also equally obvious is the fact that America's foreign policy makers, although not always in tune with public sentiment, are highly sensitive to that sentiment and are loathe to pursue for long policies that clearly run against it.

Also for better or for worse, outside the principals, the United States remains key to reaching a solution to the Palestinian-Israeli conflict. Given that American public opinion has been for too long fundamentally shaped by a coordinated and sustained effort by pro-Israel pressure groups to dehumanize the Palestinian struggle and to cast the conflict as one where Israel is merely defending itself and the Palestinians are seeking its destruction, a systematic effort to counter these pressure groups is long overdue. A healthy American policy toward the Palestinian-Israeli conflict cannot emerge as long as the US media is intimidated to remain confined to a narrow story line that serves to perpetuate and reinforce ill-founded preconceptions about the conflict.

As things stand, mainstream public opinion remains in step with the official received view. A July, 2002, survey by the Harris Poll indicates that 42% of Americans polled blame Palestinians for the conflict, while only 9% of them blame the Israelis. One year ago, only 26% of Americans blamed the Palestinians, while 14% blamed the Israelis. A CNN/USA poll conducted in May, 2002, revealed that 49% of respondents said that their sympathies lied with the Israelis, while only 15% said that they lied with the Palestinians. In August of 2001, those numbers were 41% and 13%, respectively.[33]

These surveys, among many others, demonstrate that American public opinion has by and large accepted the Israeli narrative, has internalized it, and views the conflict throw its narrow confines.

But these same surveys indicate something encouraging as well: that American public opinion is also concerned with the welfare of the Palestinians and is not wholly unsympathetic to their aspirations.[34] In a May 2002 Gallop poll, for instance, participants were asked, "Do you favor or oppose the establishment of an independent Palestinian state on the West Bank and the Gaza strip?", 48% answered that they would favor it, while only 27% said they would oppose it. In a CNN-USA TODAY poll conducted in June, 2002, participants were asked: "Do you favor or oppose the establishment of an independent Palestinian state on the West Bank if the Palestinian government demonstrates that it can end the suicide bombings in Israel?" 74% answered "favor", while only 18% said they would oppose it.[35]

More telling are surveys that indicate that American public opinion is not always wholly in tune with official policy. In a July, 2002, CBS poll, to the following question: "The Palestinians are scheduled to hold an election in 2003. If Yasir Arafat is re-elected, should the U.S. still refuse to meet with him, or should the U.S. meet with him?", 53% of the respondents answered with "Meet with him".[36]

More surprising still is the finding that "nearly 40 percent of Americans consider the violence committed by Israel against Palestinians to be terrorism, according to an ABC News poll. The Israeli lobby's pundits have for weeks argued relentlessly that Israel is merely fighting terrorism alongside Uncle Sam. Yet 4 out of 10 Americans think Israel is conducting terrorism in the West Bank."

What these findings indicate is the central importance of educating the American public about the conflict. What seems to be well-grounded American public support for Israel is in fact a mere reflection of the received narrative, time and again reinforced by such media practices as headlining Israeli violence against Palestinians as "retaliations" and "responses", by time and again front-paging large photographs of suicide attacks against Israelis, but rarely doing the same for the sniper killing by Israelis of stone-throwing Palestinian boys, house demolitions, bombings of civilian populations, etc.

Indeed, a sign that the American people are getting weary of the Israeli story line and are beginning to question it is the finding by a June, 2002, CNN/USA Today/Gallup poll which showed that the number of Americans who believe the US supports Israel too much has climbed since October, 2001, from 29% saying that the US gives too much support to Israel, to 43%.[37]

The opportunity to bring about a major change in how the public views the conflict does indeed exist. In spite of a timid media unwilling or unable to cover the conflict beyond a narrative that presents Israelis as acting out of self-defense—at times with misguided "heavy-handedness", but defensive all the same—the American people are clearly willing to think on their own and out of the usual box.

The American public is receptive to the truth and is willing to challenge received views and revise its perceptions according to what it knows.

—August 25, 2002

Israel and the US not one and the same

Here is something worth repeating: Israel is a foreign country. Israel is not an extension of the United States, not a state or a province: Israel is a foreign sovereign power, with its own military, its own intelligence services, its own economy, its own priorities and its own interests.

To be sure, Israel owes a great deal to this country—not only financially and militarily, but politically as well. Israel receives billions of dollars annually from the United States, both in economic and military aid, and enjoys the all mighty US veto at the United Nations Security Council (almost always the lone veto). But all the same, Israel is a foreign country, and this trivial fact needs to be repeated.

This basic fact is worth repeating because for all intents and purposes, Israel is rarely looked upon, either by our government or by the American public, as a foreign entity.

Often, we are led to believe that the interests of Israel are one and the same with the interests of the United States, that what is good for Israel is good for the United States, and vice versa. The latest illustration of this proposition is the intense lobbying that is taking place now by the Israeli government over the war against Iraq: Israel very badly wants the United States to attack Israel and is egging on the hawks within the Bush Administration to launch a "pre-emptive attack"—not that the Rumsfelds and the Wolfowitzs of the Bush administration need any prodding.

But what is also worth noting is that while the United States seems to believe that Israel is an extension of itself, Israel on the other hand is very clear-eyed about the nature of its relationship with its benefactor. Israel keeps its own interests well in focus and never confuses them with those of the United States. This fact was vividly illustrated after September 11, when Ariel Sharon flatly rebuffed president Bush's plea for Israel to calm things down and start talking to Yasir Arafat, so that the President can build his anti-terror coalition. "This is not the time to talk to Arafat," Mr. Sharon's response came on September 16, 2001, not more than a week after September 11. While even the Iranians had pledged cooperation, Israel had no problems saying "no".

Another example of how Israel does not confuse its interests with those of the United States, is the slap on the face that president Bush received (and seems to have nicely absorbed) when Ariel Sharon again said "no" back in March of this year to the demand that Israel withdraw from Palestinian territory re-invaded during Operation Defensive Shield. Mr. Sharon said that he would think about it, and then went ahead and did what he thought was right for his own agenda, even after president Bush kept demanding, then asking, then suggesting, that Mr. Sharon withdraw.

Other examples illustrating the fact that Israel has its own priorities and does not confuse them with those of the United States abound. Remember Jonathan Jay Pollard, the American recruited to spy for Israel and caught red-handed outside the Israeli embassy back in 1985? U.S. officials called the operation but "one link in an organized and well-financed Israeli espionage ring operating within the United States." Attorney Joseph diGenova said back in 1998: "Pollard ranks among the four most serious cases of national security damage in the history of this country…Nothing matches what he did in terms of the compromise of the technical intelligence capability of this country and he put at risk human lives."

Another shocking example that illustrates that Israel has always kept a clear-headed view of its own interests, even at the expense not only of American interests, but of the very lives of American soldiers, is the attack by Israel in 1967, on international waters, on the USS Liberty near Gaza. The attack resulted in the death of 34 sailors and the wounding of 172. To this day Israel claims that the attack was a mistake, but not one member of the surviving USS Liberty crew, or anyone who has studied what happened, believes that there is even a remote chance that the attack was mistaken. They are convinced that the only viable conclusion is that Israel, in single-minded pursuit of its interests, deliberately attacked the Liberty and meant to sink it.

And so now Ariel Sharon wants us to invade Iraq so that he can, in the mayhem of war and given "the new realities on the ground," implement his "final solution": transferring as many Palestinians out of the West Bank and Gaza and into other Arab countries. Far fetched? Not really, considering that even the Majority

Leader of the US Congress went on the record on May 1st of this year, saying the following: "There are many Arab nations that have many hundreds of thousands of acres of land and—and soil and property and opportunity to create a Palestinian state."

The interests of Israel are not one and the same with the interests of the United States. Israel is a foreign country. President Bush likes to keep his reality simple. You can't get simpler than that.

—August 30, 2002 (The Palestine Chronicle)

The Vietnam lesson—again!

The whole world (minus Israel) is praying that we don't go to war against Iraq. But we probably will: the die is cast, and it is only a matter of time now—unless we massively mobilize to stop what can only be described as a horrible act of madness.

To begin with, the propaganda season is in full swing: how interesting and convenient that all of a sudden, out of nowhere, a man approaches CNN and leads them to a large cache of tapes in exchange for a few thousand dollars. How convenient that the tapes would contain recordings of instructions on how to make chemical weapons, and, to boot, scenes of a helpless puppy yelping in agony under a deadly gaseous cloud. And how strange that the government would make no fuss over freely airing the content of those tapes, when it all but arrested CNN executives for airing portions of Al-Jazeera's bin Laden tapes last year. Wouldn't the terrorists who were apt to decode hidden messages from bin Laden be liable to pick up a couple of pointers on making a bomb or two? Apparently not.

Moreover, it is now becoming clearer by the day that Saudi Arabia is no longer willing to keep US bases on its soil for much longer. The political overhead at home is becoming so enormous that the Saudi government, taking a rare step, publicly announced that it will not give the United States permission to launch attacks against Iraq from Saudi soil. In other words, the United States needs to find a new home for its Saudi base. So, what better solution than to plop them right there in Iraq, a much better strategic position (and the weather is much nicer) than the Saudi desert, flanked by arch-enemies Iran in the east and Syria in the west, and long-time allies Turkey in the north and Kuwait and Saudi Arabia in the south?

But perhaps the best indication that we are going to war is the fact that president Bush has all but openly said that we are going in. Egged on by a team drunk with the myth of the "painless" victories of Desert Storm and the war in Afghanistan, they feel that they can easily pull it off a third time.

But maybe we should be superstitious instead of starry-eyed. Perhaps just as the third war was not a charmer with Vietnam, after the "successes" of World War Two and Korea, this war also may turn out to be an agonizing, protracted nightmare that will end badly for us. The similarities are certainly alarming: our involvement in Viet Nam was sold (though not for long) to the American public as part of a global struggle against the evil of the day back then, "the communist menace". Today, the war against Iraq is being explained (and loosely at that) in terms of our global struggle against the evil of today, "terror". Back then, we had the FBI's J Edgar Hoover uprooting and exposing Communists left and right, and keeping a close tab on anyone who rocked the boat; today, we have Attorney General John Ashcroft, who seems to have already outdone Hoover by imprisoning for months, and without formally charging them, hundreds of Americans simply on the suspicion that they could be valuable "material witnesses". Also back then we were dragged into Vietnam by a young, inexperienced president who was ill-advised by his secretary of Defense, Robert McNamara, a hawk, but a man with no real military experience. Our president today is also advised by a hawk, Donald Rumsfeld, who also happens to have very little military experience.

But perhaps we should remember now, before it is too late, the biggest lesson that came out of Vietnam: that our government should have listened to the people rather than to the hawks who knew very little about real war and were willing to put in harm's way not their own sons and daughters but those of ordinary Americans. The American people were right all along then. We had no business forcing our will on others when the threat against us was based on an unproven theory. Today, we have no business invading a country when the threat against us is once again based on a theory that has yet to be proven.

—September 1, 2002 (MediaMonitors.net)

To defeat terror, eradicate tyranny

Here we are, one year after the attacks of 9/11, and probably the only thing we know for certain right now is that today there is more resentment and anger around the world against the United States than there was prior to that fateful day.

To be sure, during the weeks and even months following the attacks, a genuine feeling of empathy and compassion for Americans prevailed across the globe. The egregious crimes shocked the world—many for the first time—into viewing Americans as flesh-and-blood, vulnerable human beings rather than indestructible Hollywood cyborgs. "They are like us, and they are suffering," was the breathless realization, to the point that even the snobbish French newspaper Le Monde dropped its usual subtle ironies and exclaimed simply, "We are all Americans!"

But today, Americans are again—and perhaps more than ever before—viewed as superhuman aliens: militarily, the United States is at least one order of magnitude stronger than the next military power, but more importantly, the United States government is now openly committed to a policy that flouts international law and the very idea of multilateral agreements and cooperation. Sadly, rather than draw from the immense well of sympathy that sprung after 9/11, and build on the firm ground of compassion and the wisdom of lost innocence, the United States decided that it MUST put humpty-dumpty back together, that it MUST show the world that America is bigger and stronger than ever, and mightier than everyone else, that it may once have been caught off guard, that it may once have been vulnerable, but that now its mission is to ensure that no one would dare again cross its path, and that if it must, it will erase from the face of this planet every single source of danger, present or potential.

But let's for a moment imagine that instead of waging a military campaign in Afghanistan and then clamoring for another war in Iraq, the US had embarked on a different path. Let's imagine that the Bush team had declared that since the perpetrators of 9/11 had been the direct mutant product of authoritarian regimes that never allowed any form of dissent, that practiced torture routinely, that treated their women as half adults and as objects, that allowed no real freedom of expression—let's imagine that the US had declared that given the fact that the nihilistic monsters of 9/11 could never have emerged were it not for the brutal regimes of Egypt and Saudi Arabia, then the US was no longer going to coddle, support, and arm those two regimes, but that instead it was holding them directly responsible for the actions of their citizens, and that Americans would from now on not rest until both of those regimes, then others like them, became full-fledged democracies, respectful of the human and civil rights of their citizens, as certified by Amnesty International, Human Rights Watch, and the United Nations Human Rights Commission. Let's imagine that instead of waging a military "war against terror", the United States had mobilized the international community in a determined campaign to rid the world of tyrannies and rogue states that breed through their actions the nihilistic terrorism we saw on 9/11.

How would the world have reacted, and more importantly, would we be today closer to dismantling the terror network?

To be sure, any regime targeted by such a policy would cry foul and interference: how dare the Americans violate the integrity of a sovereign nation? But what is also certain is that, if the Americans were to have formulated their new policy by pointing to the barbarity with which such regimes treat political dissidents, from secular challengers to Muslim activists and fundamentalists, and then firmly demanded that such barbarity must stop immediately, the deep well of sympathy that erupted after 9/11 would have further swelled with admiration: the Americans are not only human, the downtrodden would have cheered, but have now understood what it feels like to be violated and are at long last standing up for what we admire the most about the American ideal—its love for freedom and justice, and its commitment to the principles of democracy and the rule of law.

And so the world would have said, "America is turning a new page, away from its heedless hypocrisy and its double talk, and is now embarked on a new mission, informed by the basic realization that if you want to cure a disease, tend to its causes."

But instead, here we are, our commitment to democracy in tatters, our respect for international law a sham, with dictators and warmongers of all denominations, from Algeria to Israel, from Russia to Zimbabwe, piggy-backing on "the war against terror" to settle political scores, snuff out the faintest spark of dissent, engage in ethnic cleansing, and brutalize minorities. Now, to the rest of the world, the United States looks more than ever before like a super-cyborg run amok—a Robocop—heedless, unfeeling, consumed by its own power, and possessed by the idea of smashing and destroying all that stands in its path, the better to ensure that the very memory of America's vulnerability—its humanity—is banished from everyone's thoughts. If bin Laden is still alive, he can't be too unhappy.

The world can be made not only as safe as it was prior to 9/11, but much safer. How? By promoting the very values that moved people around the world to stand in mourning and solidarity with America on that tragic day, one year ago.

—September 9, 2002 (The Detroit News)

Blind journalism, American style

A 15-year-old boy threw stones at a tank that was besieging the headquarters of a national leader. A soldier shot him in the head from short range, killing him…A soldier in an undercover unit gave hot pursuit to a boy of about nine who had been throwing stones, shot him from behind and killed him—Gideon Levy, Ha'aretz, "The message from high command," February 10, 2002

On July 22nd, 2002, only a couple of hours after a one-ton bomb was dropped by an Israeli F-16 jet fighter on a densely-populated area in Gaza, killing the head of the Hamas military wing, along with 9 sleeping children and five other civilians, CNN's Aaron Brown opened his NewsNight broadcast with the following statement: "it seems clear that either the planning was horrible, or that the missile missed [its] target, or the Israelis simply didn't care who they killed if they got their man, a Hamas military leader. At the risk of provoking an e-mail barrage, we reject the latter possibility. We don't believe the Israeli government would risk killing a couple of hundred people in order to maybe—maybe—get one guy." [38]

Mr. Brown did indeed receive a barrage of protest emails following his remarks, but on the very next day he made it clear that he was not impressed. On the July 23rd program, Mr. Brown followed up with this: "We said last night, and we believe still, the Israeli government would not launch an assassination attack like the one last night if it believed there was a risk that hundreds of civilians would die. We received scores of notes on that line alone. My mind, despite your best efforts, remains unchanged." [39] In other words, at worst, Israel can be accused of committing "tragic errors", and errors are just that, errors. [40] Even callous disregard will not be seriously considered. The fact that these "tragic errors" have been taking place literally on a daily basis, and that they are clear instances of violations of the Geneva Conventions Pertaining to the Treatment of Civilian Populations, which explicitly prohibits any "attack which may be expected to cause incidental loss of civilian life, injury to civilians, damage to civilian objects, or a combination thereof", is beside the point. Unlike the suicide bombers, we are told, the Israelis are not out to simply kill civilians. The proof being that after some of these "tragic errors" (and only the most egregious ones, and among those, only

107

the ones that elicit an outcry from the world an a faint frown from the US administration), Israeli government spokesmen express regret ("our hearts are heavy," is Shimon Peres's favorite expression on this score). But as veteran Middle East reporter for the Independent Robert Fisk bitterly notes, forgiving such "tragic errors" is like "forgiving an arsonist who burned your mother to death in a crowded hotel—on the grounds that he had not known your mother was in the building when he set fire to it."[41]

That a journalist would have certain preconceptions about how the world works is of course inevitable: journalists are human beings, and human beings have opinions and operate within a world where a lot is taken for granted and accepted as such. But at the heart of what professional journalists do—what makes them professional seekers of the truth—is their constant struggle to stand above their preconceptions and prejudices. What is shocking about Aaron Brown's remarks is not the fact that he was willing to give the benefit of the doubt to the Israelis, or even that he said out loud what he felt, but rather that he would openly terminate an investigative line on an assumption. Journalists are not supposed to start a story with a conclusion, let alone a conclusion drawn from an unlikely assumption (Ariel Sharon supervised the killing of 17,500, not just "a couple of hundred," Lebanese civilians in his pursuit of the PLO in 1982). And indeed, as his subsequent questioning of official Israeli spokesmen and unofficial apologists of Israeli policies clearly illustrated, the mere possibility that the Israelis did not care about the civilians they knew they would be killing in their attacks was never seriously pursued by Mr. Brown. As for the notion that Ariel Sharon may have deliberately dropped the one-ton bomb in a residential area to provoke Hamas and to derail the unilateral cease-fire that was allegedly being worked out by the Palestinians—a theory practically universally accepted as the only plausible explanation for the timing of the attack and its raw aggression against a civilian population—that possibility was outright eliminated from the outset; it was literally unmentionable, beyond contemplation. (And indeed, suicide bombings followed the raid, as expected.) The possible realm of acceptable explanations was restricted, as Mr. Brown openly explained to his audience, to either "the planning was horrible, or…the missile missed [its] target", and hence so were the questions and the lines of inquiry that followed.

Aaron Brown if of course no exception, and his example is notable only in its naked openness. Examples of such gingerly, second nature winnowing of reality abound in the US media's coverage of the Palestinian-Israeli conflict. Another startling and no less shocking illustration of such deep-seated commitment to a narrow worldview that by definition eliminates what is within the legitimate field of investigation for reporters of the Middle East conflict, is the reaction of the US media to a story published in the October 2001 issue of Harper's Magazine by veteran New York Times reporter Chris Hedges.[42] The piece was titled "A Gaza Diary" and alleged that Israeli soldiers not only deliberately targeted stone throwing Palestinian children, but in fact routinely taunted them and incited them, only to shoot them when they started throwing stones at them. On October 31, 2001, appearing on NPR's Fresh Air, Mr. Hedges reiterated his accusations even more bluntly:

"And I walked out towards the dunes and they were—the—over the loudspeaker from an Israeli army Jeep on the other side of the electric fence they were taunting these kids. And these kids started to throw rocks. And most of these kids were 10, 11, 12 years old. And, first of all, the rocks were the size of a fist. They were being hurled towards a Jeep that was armor-plated. I doubt they could even hit the Jeep. And then I watched the soldiers open fire. And it was—I mean, I've seen kids shot in Sarajevo. I mean, snipers would shoot kids in Sarajevo. I've seen death squads kill families in Algeria or El Salvador. But I'd never seen soldiers bait or taunt kids like this and then shoot them for sport. It was—I just—even now, I find it almost inconceivable. And I went back every day, and every day it was the same."[43]

How did the US media react?

To this day, I have yet to see a single editorial that raised the issue of IDF soldiers deliberately shooting children. Evidence that such shooting occurs, and regularly, has been extensively documented not only by journalists, but by human rights organizations from Israel, Europe, and the United States.[5] Physicians for Human Rights have more than once concluded that "[Israeli] soldiers are specifically aiming at peoples' heads"; the Israeli group, B'tselem, reported in October 2001 that "the IDF continues to employ a policy of 'an easy trigger-finger' and demonstrates a disregard for human life"; in a joint statement given on April 7, 2002, Amnesty International and the International Commission of Jurists declared, "Palestinians have been killed attempting to reach hospitals for routine medical care. Such abuses raise not simply humanitarian issues: they are serious violations of international humanitarian law"; Human Rights Watch issued a report on May 3, 2002 concerning Israeli atrocities in Jenin, stating in part, "[Palestinian] civilians [in Jenin] were killed willfully or unlawfully [by the Israeli military]....[which] used Palestinian civilians as 'human shields' and used indiscriminate and excessive force....The abuses we documented in Jenin are extremely serious, and in some cases appear to be war crimes"; in an interview with Ha'aretz reporter Amira Hass, an Israeli sniper described the commands he receives from his superiors: "Twelve and up, you're allowed to shoot. That's what they tell us" ("So," responded the reporter "according to the IDF, [the appropriate minimum age group at which to shoot] is 12?" the soldier replied, "According to what the IDF says to its soldiers. I don't know if this is what the IDF says to the media"); from the BBC, July 5, 2002: "The BBC has obtained video footage which appears to show an incident in the West Bank city of Jenin two weeks ago in which two Palestinian children were killed by Israeli tank fire.... the footage shows a tank firing the first of two shells, at close range, at a group of civilians who are running away."[44]

And yet, editors will simply not mention these findings, let alone openly condemn the actions they describe. Instead, they cling to the established narrative that only Palestinians deliberately target civilians in terrorist attacks. Indeed, when I contacted a member of the New York Times editorial board on the findings of Chris Hedges and asked him to explain the New York Times' silence over Hedges' report, here is what the editor had to say: "you are making too much of his Harper's piece. Chris has not been a Middle East reporter since the early 90's. He speaks neither Arabic nor Hebrew. He went to Gaza for a week a year ago and wrote a strong piece with some very disturbing allegations and conclusions. But to assert that the world should have taken what he wrote as gospel makes no sense."[45]

When I quoted Hedges to him again—i.e., "And I speak Arabic, so I'm listening over the loudspeaker to the worst curse words in Arabic, and phrases like, you know, 'All the Palestinians who live in Khan Yunis are dogs,' which is calling an Arab a dog is particularly insulting"—and suggested that he was doing nothing less than accusing one of his own reporters of outright lying, the editor's response was: "I'm not saying he's a liar. I'm saying that unless others report the same thing, we're left to wonder why. Chris studied Arabic 10 years ago or so. But he cannot work professionally in Arabic without a translator. I am certain he heard soldiers shouting kus umak and the other horrors to the kids that he reports."[46]

The fact that Mr. Hedges clearly said that he spoke Arabic, that he was listening over the loudspeaker rather than having someone translate to him, would not budge the editor's refusal to believe that IDF soldiers would perpetrate the atrocities Hedges was bluntly reporting. As for evidence beyond what Hedges was reporting, I did provide the editor with a long list of quotes from respected human rights organizations that stated without ambiguity that IDF soldiers do deliberately target civilians (from which I drew for my quotes above). But, to this day, the editor remains serenely unmoved. In his reality, Israelis do not commit such atrocities, and no amount of evidence is going to rattle his well-protected conceptual cage.

An even more egregious example of denial that trespasses into the territory of breathless hypocrisy is the March 17, 2002, column by Nolan Finley, editorial page editor of The Detroit News, in which he wrote, "The ugly little secret of the Middle East conflict is that a favorite target of Palestinian terrorists are the children, teen-agers and young adults of Israel."[47] In that piece, Mr. Finley cited no reports, no findings or investigations, no official statements from human rights organizations or respected journalists, showing that Palestinian terrorists "appear to be intentionally killing Israel's kids." And yet, he had no qualms titling his piece, "Israel's children are the target of Middle East terror campaign". I point to Nolan Finley's column only because I myself published an op-ed on December 9, 2001, on the very pages that Mr. Finley edits, in which I extensively quoted from Chris Hedges' piece. When Mr. Finley's piece appeared, I sent him Chris Hedges report, a transcript of his October 30 appearance on NPR's Fresh Air, and the above mentioned long list of quotes from human rights organizations showing that Israelis do target civilians and children, but again, to no avail. To this day, Mr. Finley has yet to respond, let alone write a column condemning the well-documented practice (and some say policy) by the IDF of intentionally killing civilians.

The refusal to even consider the possibility that the IDF does routinely target civilians is of course not confined to editorial boards. The paradigm that views Israelis as at worst unintentionally or mistakenly killing civilians (with "stray bullets" and "errant shells") is well engrained in the news reporting of all the major newspapers, resulting in coverage that reports suicide bombings with blaring, banner-headlines and large above the fold front page photographs, while the killing of Palestinian civilians (even children) is covered with little fanfare, rarely highlighted on the front page, let alone given a banner headline or an above the fold photograph. Here are some examples:

On Friday, June 21,2002, IDF soldiers opened fire on the Jenin marketplace in broad day light, killing four Palestinians—three children and a schoolteacher—and wounding dozens. The IDF claimed that the soldiers erred in firing the shells and said that it was opening an investigation into the matter. In a survey of 20 US papers, Palestine Media Watch discovered the following: (1) out of the 20 papers surveyed, only one paper, the Seattle Times, showed a front-page picture of the attack; (2) out of the 20, 11 ran a front-page story on the shelling, and of the 11 that ran a front page of the story, 5 reported in their headline as a matter of fact that the shelling was "a mistake"—as in, "Israeli tanks mistakenly kill 4 civilians in West Bank" (San Francisco Chronicle)—while the other six qualified the description of "error" as a claim from the IDF and not a simple fact; and (3) of the 11 than ran a front page story, only 4 mentioned in the headline that 3 out of the 4 victims were children.[48]

Or take the July 22, 2002, Gaza bombing, in which a Hamas leader was killed along with 9 sleeping children and 5 more civilians. Of the 17 papers whose July 23 front page we examined, only only 6 ran a front page, above the fold picture depicting the aftermath of the attack, and only two mentioned in the headline that children were among those killed: The Los Angeles Times and the San Diego Union Tribune.[49]

Speaking of pictures, one the most vivid visual illustrations of how the media will simply not highlight Palestinian suffering to the same extent that it does Israeli suffering is the shocking disproportion between the number of above the fold front-page photographs the Philadelphia Inquirer has run depicting Israelis after a Palestinian attack (usually suicide bombings) and Palestinians after an Israeli attack.

Between March 28, 2002 and August 1, 2002, the Philadelphia Inquirer published 13 above the fold photographs depicting the Israeli human toll after suicide bombings, while during that same period, it published only 1 above the fold picture depicting the Palestinian human toll of Israeli attacks on Palestinians.[50] The 13 pictures depicting Israeli suffering occupied 87.61% of all above the fold pictures on the conflict depicting human suffering after specific attacks; Palestinian human suffering occupied only 12.39%. Moreover, during that same period, the Philadelphia Inquirer published 10 front-page photos showing Palestinians. Of those 10, 6 depicted militants, suicide bombers, and would be suicide bombers, while the other 4 showed the Palestinians as civilians. Also, out of those 10 pictures, 3 were above the fold; significantly all 3 pictures depicted suicide bombers and accused militants. Also quite telling is the fact that during that same period, the Inquirer front-paged only two pictures showing Israelis in a slightly negative light (one showing soldiers patrolling the streets and one showing a soldier yelling at civilians), and both were small in size and below the fold. These findings are the more significant since the period of this analysis starts with the re-invasion of the West Bank and coincides with the beginning of Operation Defensive Shield, during which 497 Palestinians were killed, according to the conservative estimate of the United Nations.[51]

When confronted with the findings of the analysis, the Inquirer's Foreign Desk editor, Ned Warwick, first tried to justify the lopsided results by claiming that pictures out of the West Bank were hard to come by. When we pointed out to him that the Inquirer did routinely run some good pictures, but only buried inside the paper, Mr. Warwick agreed that it was "strange" and that he would "certainly look into it with our photo editors". Needless to say, the Inquirer has done nothing to remedy the situation since then (the July 22 bombing, for instance, was treated with a below the fold, small picture). Worse still is the fact that the Inquirer's editor in chief, Walker Lundy, has been answering queries from people who have asked him about the report by writing, "We have published a variety of photos this year. Since we don't keep count, I have no idea what the number is, but I doubt their figures are accurate."[52] The Inquirer has yet to publicly challenge our findings or to conduct their own survey.

The vocabulary used in covering the conflict is also quite indicative of the extent to which the US media is entrenched in the paradigm that views Israelis as engaged in self-defense and never intentionally targeting civilians.

A Lexis-Nexis analysis for the words "retaliation" or "retaliate" within the text of news reports filed from Israel/Palestine and published in the Washington Post over a 19 month period (from the start of the Intifada up to May 2002) revealed the following: 32 news stories were found that used the words "retaliation" or "retaliate" somewhere in the text and not in the context of a quotation. Of those, 31 instances were specifically in reference to Israeli actions and were presented as facts rather than as points of view or as justifications offered by the Israeli government. Only in one instance was the word "retaliation" used as it should be: as a claim made by Israeli government spokespeople and not as an uncontested fact.[53]

In other words, according to the Washington Post, Israel never initiates violent actions, but only "retaliates"; that is, Israel is always acting out of self-defense, never engaging in calculated acts of aggression.

Another Lexis-Nexis database search for the words "terror" and "vigilante" within the text of news reports filed from Israel and published in the Washington Post for the 17 months following the start of the Intifada revealed that the word "terror" was used exclusively to describe Palestinian violence and "vigilante" exclusively to describe Israeli settler violence. Again, the implication and the defining paradigm being that only Palestinians engage in the intentional, calculated killing of civilians, while Israelis only react, sometimes using "heavy-handed" methods, but never deliberately target their victims.[54]

Commitment to the prevailing paradigm is of course not confined to the printed press. The electronic media is just as guilty. For Dan Fisher, MSNBC'S ombudsman, a veteran of the Middle East dating back to the first Intifada, the possibility that the Israeli military is engaged in terror is not worth considering: "I really dislike the euphemism 'collateral damage'," he wrote in a March 2002 column, "but in fact there are almost bound to be civilian casualties in such a conflict. The moral question, it seems to me, is not whether the opposing military force is guilty of 'terrorism' in such a situation, but whether it takes adequate precautions to avoid noncombatant casualties. And that, clearly, is a very tough thing for news reporters to judge."[55]

Even more blunt and certainly not as reflective is CNN's Eason Jordan, who, in his July 3, 2002, appearance on PBS's NewsHour, explained that "there's a big difference...between what's happening in Israel and what's happening in the Palestinian territories, because while it's disputable whether Israel is targeting civilians, there's certainly no irrefutable evidence of that in the territories. There's no doubt that suicide bombers are going into Israel and intentionally killing civilians at random."[56] When a team from Palestine Media Watch met with him on July 10, 2002, and presented him with an extensive report quoting dozens of Human Rights organizations, including American and Israeli groups, along with respected journalists on the ground, showing beyond any doubt that the IDF does intentionally target civilians, Mr. Jordan refused to even entertain the possibility that Israelis do indeed target civilians. The evidence did not matter.[57]

As I said, if such opinions were confined to personal behavior and outlook, no one should be bothered. But when preconceptions begin to dictate, and openly so, what is investigated and what is ignored, what questions are asked and what questions are dismissed (or are never even entertained), what is deemed outrageous and what is not, then red flags should be raised, especially when the evidence is compelling that the preconceptions are ill-founded or outright wrong. In the case of CNN, Eason Jordan openly drew the distinction between Palestinian and Israeli actions to justify why CNN had decided to run a weeklong, five-part series (June 24-28) on Israeli victims of Palestinian attacks, but had declined to do the same for Palestinian victims of Israeli attacks. CNN has also erected an extensive web gallery of all Israeli victims of Palestinian attacks since January 1, 2002, but has refused to do the same for Palestinian victims, again on grounds that the first were killed intentionally, while the latter were not. (I am here of course setting aside the obvious question: why should the intention of the perpetrators determine whether or not or how extensively one should cover the suffering of the victims?)[58] Indeed, as if to ensure that there remained no doubt that CNN does practice double standards, after two months and a half of protest from many groups (a running petition endorsed by 79 organizations is periodically presented to CNN), CNN established what it calls a "Palestinian Fatalities" gallery that covers exactly 3 days—August 29, 30, 31, and September 1, 2002, and displays a total of 10 photographs, not one of which shows the face of a Palestinian "fatality"! It is of course significant to note that the word chosen was "fatality" and not "victim". The Israeli gallery is called, "Victims of terror" and lists hundreds of photographs, all of them the faces of victims of suicide bombings.[59]

The examples I cite here—CNN's Aaron Brown, The New York Times' editorial board, Nolan Finley of the Detroit News, The Washington Post's Foreign Desk, Ned Warwick of the Philadelphia Inquirer, Dan Fisher of MSNBC, Eason Jordan of CNN—are not the exception but the rule. US coverage of the Middle East conflict suffers from a debilitating commitment to a paradigm that can no longer hold together. The evidence is massive that the IDF does systematically target civilians, at least as a matter of practice, and probably as a matter of unspoken policy (Ha'aretz 's Gideon Levy speaks of "The message from high command").

Unless and until American journalists free themselves from the blinders they have decided to put on when converging the Middle East conflict, until they embrace all of reality with all of unpleasant possibilities, we will continue to suffer reporting that avoids the obvious and often presents as obviously true what is misleading, incomplete, or outright false.

—September 29, 2002 (Editor&Publisher)[60]

Project Censorship

Daniel Pipes is not even bothering anymore with his usual smoke and mirrors: the Council On American-Islamic Relations, one of the most respected Muslim advocacy groups in the United States, is the equivalent of the KKK, Mr. Pipes announced in public a few weeks ago during a conference televised by C-SPAN; last year, at the American Jewish Congress, he told his audience, "I worry very much from the Jewish point of view that the presence, and increased stature, and affluence, and enfranchisement of America Muslims…will present true dangers to American Jews"; and just last month, Mr. Pipes led a campaign to block Palestinian spokesman Hanan Ashrawi from delivering her keynote address at a symposium on the September 11 terrorist attacks. Her appearance at the event was "a grievous error", Mr. Pipes complained. "Simply put, the United States is engaged in a war on terror, and Mrs. Ashrawi is on the side of America's enemies," he said, then added, not mincing his words: "We should work so that this type of anti-American spokeswoman is not welcome on American campuses."

Of course, anyone who has heard Hanan Ashrawi speak, who is familiar with her stand on the Palestinian-Israeli conflict, who has read her articles on the crisis and her best-seller book on the Oslo negotiations, knows that Pipes' attacks against Mrs. Ashrawi are as unseemly as they are groundless. Mrs. Ashrawi, who has for years quietly headed a Palestinian NGO, The Palestinian Initiative for the Promotion of Global Dialog and Democracy, to build a democratic infrastructure from the grassroots, on the ground, without fanfare and hype, is the exact kind of leader that President Bush ostensibly said the Palestinians should seek out and elevate to the top: leaders that believe in peaceful, non-violent resistance, and in clean, open government—i.e., in dialog and democracy. But all that is troubling noise for Mr. Pipes. Hanan Ashrawi is in his eyes first and foremost a dangerous enemy, the more dangerous because she is an effective counter-voice to the glib and media savvy spokesmen of Israel, official or unofficial. Mrs. Ashrawi, a PhD graduate of the University of Virginia, knows American culture and can connect with Americans, and is charismatic to boot. Her understated, principled firmness, her refusal to take cheap shots, her dignity and eloquence, and her disarming, wide smile, have rendered her a formidable spokesperson. Priority number one for Mr. Pipes and his like is to shut her off: to keep Americans safely away from this compelling defender of Palestinian rights.

Mr. Pipes is of course only the tip of a much wider effort. A long-standing strategy by pro-Israel interest groups consists in working relentlessly not only to promote and defend their point of view, but also to eliminate anything that runs counter the established narrative, whereby Israel is presented as a victim and the Palestinians as one-dimensional killers set on Israel's destruction. A cornerstone of this mission is to demonize anyone who either directly undermines the narrative or proposes an alternative view of the conflict.

What is striking about this phenomenon is that it is quite unique in the American landscape of today. Other strong lobby groups, such as the National Rifle Association, the tobacco lobby, or even the pro-life, anti-abortion movement, do indeed press their case with unapologetic force and couch their arguments in constitutional and moral terms. But none of them works to consciously eliminate the mere existence of dissenting voices. All of these groups take it as a given that expressions of dissent are part and parcel of the democratic process, and proceed from that given starting point to wage their passionate battles to win the hearts and minds of the American people.

Pro-Israel groups, by contrast, violate the very core principle of democratic participation: they aim not simply to compete in the arena of open, healthy dialog, but to eliminate dissent by all means possible. Front and center in their quest to win the hearts and minds of the American people is the strategy of truncating the debate. Anyone who dares to stray too far or too prominently from the orthodox line on Israel is quickly branded a foe of Israel, and worse, beyond the pale of acceptable discourse, and therefore a target for exlcusion.

In Congress, for instance, lawmakers are loathe to even express views that deviate from the mainstream line on Israel, let alone act on them, and those who do express such heresies—especially those with signs of political vulnerability—incur the wrath of the well-organized and handsomely financed pro-Israel lobby groups and risk their very political head. In this election season, for example, such groups mobilized against Alabama's Earl Hilliard and Georgia's Cynthia McKinney and worked to unseat both. The exact contribution of these groups to the defeat of the two Congresspersons remains in some dispute. But what is important to note is that even though neither Congressman can be described as anti-Israel (they both voted repeatedly for legislation favorable to Israel), pro-Israel lobby groups nevertheless decided that since both dared to question a couple of pro-Israel bills (all of them non-binding) and since both were prominent defenders of Arab and Muslim rights, they were therefore prime candidates for attack. The fact that more than 90% of Congress is solidly toeing the pro-Israel line is clearly beside the point for pro-Israel groups, since their true agenda is not simply to ensure massive support, but more importantly to eliminate dissent.

The impulse to shut off anything that deviates from the norm as defined by pro-Israel groups is perhaps best illustrated by the relentless attacks and ugly accusations by pro Israel groups against the US media. Such attacks usually peak in ferocity when the Israeli army engages in military actions that cause widespread, visible Palestinian suffering. During the Israeli re-invasion of the West Bank back in March of this year, the images of carnage and wanton destruction emanating from Ramallah, Jenin, Tulkarem, Bethlehem, Nablus, ran the risk of shattering the image that pro-Israel groups carefully cultivate about Israel: the peace-loving country, the "only democracy in the Middle East", under assault and struggling to survive, solicitous of the welfare of Palestinians and concerned with their human rights. The images instead communicated another reality: an ugly, bloody war machine run amok, attacking civilians and destroying anything and everything Palestinian, including the computer hard disks of the education ministry and the payroll files of the agriculture ministry.

The reaction of pro-Israel groups was as violent and hysterical as it was predictable: pro-Israel groups mobilized a nation-wide push to boycott all the major media outlets for their "pro-Palestinian" coverage. "Pro-Palestinian" simply because the stories published and the images shown showed suffering Palestinians. By running stories that described the horrors of the Israeli invasion, newspapers and print periodicals were anti-Israeli abettors of terror, even anti-Semitic. (Members of the Zionist Organization of American in Philadelphia, for instance, went so far as to accuse the Philadelphia Inquirer, a Knight Ridder newspaper, of harboring pro-Nazi sympathies.) Even giant CNN, which covers the conflict with even much greater diffidence to pro-Israeli sensitivities, was threatened with cancellation by Israel's cable services and its replacement by FoxNews, an outlet that openly and unapologetically toes the official Israeli line on the conflict (they adopted the use of the expression "homicide bombing" as soon as Israel's spokesmen, followed by the Bush administration, began using the phrase).

To be sure, little financial damage was suffered by the big outlets from these boycotts, and from the reaction of editors and ombudsmen, the anti-Media campaign has generated angry resentment from foreign desks and editorial boards who take exception to such blatant attempts to intimidate them into toning down their reporting and their editorial stand. But at least in the case of one middling newspaper, the Philadelphia Inquirer, the campaign did have its intended effect. For instance, a study of the front page photographs of the Philadelphia Inquirer between March 28, 2002 and August 1, 2002 has revealed that during that period, the Inquirer ran 13 above the fold photographs showing Israeli human suffering, while only 1 photograph showing Palestinian human suffering. This was during the height of the Israeli military campaign to re-invade the West Bank, when, according to the conservative estimates of the United Nations, 497 Palestinians were killed. When asked to explain the large discrepancy, Ned Warwick, the Foreign Desk editor, offered the following explanation: photographs from the ground showing Palestinian suffering were hard to obtain! (The Inquirer routinely runs very powerful pictures of such suffering, but always buried inside the newspaper.) Another example is the Inquirer's coverage of the 30th anniversary of the Munich massacres on September 5, 2002 (the paper ran a front page story and a sports section story), but its total blackout of 20th anniversary of the Sabra and Shatila massacres. When asked about the pass the Inquirer took on the anniversary, the Foreign Desk editor again offered an unlikely explanation: they had simply forgotten, he explained, what with the Iraq situation and all. The Inquirer does have a man stationed on the ground in Israel.

An equally blatant example of the impulse to choke off the free flow of information on the conflict and silence whatever does not chime well with the pro-Israel song are the comments made by New York Post movie critic Jonathan Foreman during his April 5th appearance on CNN's NewsNight with Aaron Brown. Mr. Foreman's chief complaint was that the media were focusing too much on the Middle East and that it should instead turn its sights on other flashpoints around the world, such as Kashmir. When his host suggested that perhaps the focus on the conflict had something to do with the "confluence of American interest, economic and political American interests and the possibility of a broader war throughout the Middle East, or throughout any region in the world," Mr. Foreman simply answered with: "There's no actual sign of those Arab countries starting to make a real—have a real war with Israel". So paramount is the goal of shutting off debate that in his drive to seek it, Mr. Foreman neglected to notice that he was throwing with the bath water of ugly press the baby of Israel's PR machine: the notion that the Jewish state was under existential threat from its Arab neighbors and that therefore all is fair game in self-defense!

Also quite startling is CNN's buckling under intense pro-Israel pressure groups. On June 28, only a few days after CNN's top executives had met with Israeli officials who had threatened to shut off CNN from the Israeli cable lineup, CNN, without prior publicity or warning, began airing a weeklong series, hosted by Wolf Blitzer, on Israeli victims of suicide bombings. In conjunction with the series, CNN quickly established a gallery it titled, "The Victims of Terror" (it later turned out that the content of the CNN gallery was provided practically in toto by a pro-Israeli web site), listing the photograph, name, short bio, and the circumstance of death of every Israel victim of suicide bombing since January 1, 2002. When a petition from 79 organizations was presented to CNN, requesting that a similar series and web gallery be established for innocent Palestinian victims of Israeli attacks—or at least a gallery for the children of such attacks—CNN openly refused. The answer it gave is quite telling: Israelis are killed intentionally, while Palestinians are killed accidentally, explained CNN's Eason Jordan on the July 3rd edition of PBS's NewsHour. When confronted with compelling evidence that IDF soldiers do indeed target civilians intentionally, CNN simply ignored it. (Needless to say, CNN was hardly moved by the argument that the intention of a perpetrator of a crime should not determine whether the suffering of an innocent victim is covered or ignored.)

But perhaps the most insidious and most desperate attempt to date at shutting off voices that refuse to toe the usual line is the cyber-terror campaign that has been underway against pro-Palestinian activists for more than two months now. The campaign consists in identifying pro-Palestinian activists (e.g., heads of organizations, webmasters, writers, or active participants in pro-Palestinian mailing lists) and then sending hundreds of emails that are made to appear as if they had been sent out by the activists in question. Most of those emails contain either pro-Israeli material, crude support for pro-terrorist attacks on the US and anti-Semitic slurs against Jews, or good old obscenities. The intention is clear: to make the email addresses of the most active members of the community unwelcome by likely recipients of messages from those activists. Indeed, some, unable to sustain waves of hundreds of emails clogging their mail boxes, have done exactly that: blocked the email addresses of such activists. (The perpetrators of these cyber terrorist actions have been identified, but the authorities so far have been very slow to respond.)

No other issue on the American landscape has generated such a concerted and sustained drive by one side to limit or even eliminate the very expression of dissent by the other side as the Middle East conflict has. Pro-Israel groups, unlike other passionate organized interests, vociferously protest the very expression of opposing views and work to narrow the discourse space afforded to such views. Those who do ask for or promote a wider debate on the issue are quickly identified as the enemy, and concerted work is undertaken to silence them. This phenomenon should be alarming for those who cherish the American democratic tradition, where dissent is respected and open discussion embraced and encouraged.

Indeed, loud alarms should be sounded now, since the push has apparently crept into the last bastion of free expression: the university campus. Daniel Pipes has now established a web site named Campus Watch, http://www.campus-watch.org. Its mission? Nothing less than putting up a list of people with whom Pipes disagrees—"American scholars…[who] reject the views of most Americans and the enduring policies of the U.S. government about the Middle East"—with the intent of thereby discrediting them and subjecting them to discrimination and harassment. This of course is a chilling throwback to the McCarthy era and earlier, when such lists by self-appointed thought policemen, frequently in collaboration with local police Red Squads and anti-union employers, were widely used. These tactics, in gross violation of basic democratic principles, are now recognized to have been a shameful abuse of private and governmental power. Daniel Pipes and his friends are bringing them back. If we are determined not to let history repeat itself, we should sit up, take notice, and stop Mr. Pipes and his likes in their tracks, now, before we sink into another dark night of fear and hysteria and the unthinkable becomes acceptable reality.

—October 13, 2002

Our money, our priorities

I am not much of a cheerleader for government boondoggles to big business, but the refusal by the Air Transportation Stabilization Board (ATSB) to grant United Airlines, the nation's No. 2 airline, a loan for $2 billion to keep it afloat caught me by surprise, I must confess. The White House, so far stunningly shameless in its naked hypocrisy, could easily have argued—one might have thought—that the Airline industry is crucial to the well-being of the economy at large and that a $2 billion dollar loan is a worthwhile investment. But apparently, the political climate is so afoul of anything that smacks of corporate cronyism that even Bush had to resist the temptation.

But there is one boondoggle that seems to be hermetically immune from any political winds or sensitivities.

Just about two weeks ago, on Monday November 25, according to the Israeli newspaper Ha'aretz (the US media simply did not deem the news worthy of mention), the United States approved a request from Israel for $14 billion in aid over the next few years, above and beyond the annual $3 billion automatically given to Israel every year.

At a time when a crucial business such as the second largest airline is facing collapse, and when the White House and both houses of Congress are fully under the control of radical pro-business types, it is nothing short of stunning that within less than a span of two weeks, $14 billion would be handed out to a foreign nation, with not as much as a mention, let alone with protest or fanfare, while an enterprise vital to the US economy would be allowed to collapse, and so publicly, adding to the jitters of a market already on the verge of a nervous breakdown.

But beside being able to save United Airlines and six other of its unhappy clones—not my idea of spending our tax money wisely—here is what else those billions could help fix. According to The Children's Defense fund:

An American child is born into poverty every 43 seconds; one in five children is poor during the first three years of life—the time of greatest brain development.

Nearly 12 million children are poor, and millions are hungry, at risk of hunger, living in worst case housing, or homeless. Almost 80 percent of poor children live in working households.

An American child is born without health insurance every minute—90 percent of the nine million uninsured children live in working families.

In January 2002, when President Bush signed his "No Child Left Behind" (H.R. 1) education reform bill, he "vowed to make educating every child his number one domestic priority." And yet, the administration's 2003 budget proposed the smallest education increase in the past seven years!

The Bush administration's assault on welfare and the working poor will result in 114,000 fewer children in working families getting federal child care assistance despite long child care waiting lists in many states.[61]

With this in mind, here are some more facts to put the $14 billion grant to Israel in its proper perspective: Israel's per capita GDP is $20,000—higher than that of Spain ($18,900) and Portugal ($17,300), twice that of oil rich Saudi Arabia ($10,600), more than twice that of Russia ($8,300), ten times more than that of Pakistan ($2,100) and India ($2,500). And remember Afghanistan and how the US was going to make sure that "never again" will we allow it to collapse back into chaos? Israel's per capita GPD is more than twenty times that of Afghanistan ($800). I don't recall Bush signing any billions of dollars away to help restore Afganistan's devastated infrastructure.[62]

As for how much Israel's entitlement for next year will be: for 2003, the Bush administration is proposing that Israel receive $2.76 billion in foreign aid, with $2.1 billion in military grants from the Department of Defense and $600 million in Economic Support Funds from the State Department.

And if you thought the heady days of Enron and WorldCom of diverting funds and playing with the books were behind us, think twice: the Bush team is proposing an additional $28 million to go to Israel for the purchase U.S. manufactured counter terrorism equipment.[63] Not a bad idea: if you are going to launder money, do it through the one country than no one will dare question you over.

—December 6, 2002

Outrage should not need green light from the White House

When Trent Lott uttered his infamous words of praise for Strom Thurmund last December 5, he was probably counting on the one thing you can take to the bank nowadays in Washington: a moribund media that will gloss over anything, no matter how outrageous, as long as the White House gives it a pass.

So, when President Bush lauded Sen. Thurmund, saying, "his patriotism, courage and lifetime dedication to South Carolina and his nation will always be remembered,"[64] when he feted him at the White House the day after his 100th birthday, and planned on attending ceremonies on December 12 at Andrews Air Force Base, where the Air Force was to name its 100th C-17 cargo plane the 'Spirit of Strom Thurmond' (the ceremonies went ahead as planned, minus the President)[65], the whole Lott thing was literally treated by the media as an unremarkable non-event.

Until, that is, the storm erupted in full force on Friday the 13th, appropriately enough for Lott, when President Bush decided that it was time to publicly and harshly rebuke Senator Lott for his remarks.

Up to that point, the media was at best counting on milking the story for no more than a few days, until the next "real" crisis erupts. "The story has no legs", Rush Limbaugh opined wishfully and self-servingly, and amazingly enough, the mainstream media seemed to think so, too.

Now, after Bush's blunt speech, the Lott crisis has become "Breaking News" and "Special Bulletin" material, with frantic speculation over Lott's impending resignation from his leadership position, if not his seat altogether.

But the media's sorry handling of the Lott affaire is not the exception, but the rule.

Here are a few more outrages that have gone by wholly unnoticed by the US media simply because the White House has either deemed them not worthy of its moral indignation or has itself perpetrated them.

On May 1 of this year, as a guest of MSNBC's Hardball with Chris Matthews, House Republican Majority Leader Dick Armey (R-TX) spoke on the record for the transfer of Palestinian populations from the West Bank and Gaza to other Arab countries and the permanent annexation of those lands by Israel.

When Chris Matthews asked Mr. Armey point-blank, "you believe that the Palestinians who are now living on the West Bank should get out of there?", Mr. Armey answered without mincing his words, "Yes." Then he elaborated: "There are many Arab nations that have many hundreds of thousands of acres of land and—and soil and property and opportunity to create a Palestinian state."[66]

For those who take the Geneva Conventions seriously, Dick Armey was calling for the transfer of populations—pure and unadulterated ethnic cleansing—a straightforward violation of Sections 1 and 4 of Article 12, and at least technically an instance of genocide. "People suspected of acts of genocide," the Conventions stipulate, "may be tried by a national tribunal in the territory where the acts were committed or by a properly constituted international tribunal whose jurisdiction is recognized by the state or states involved."[67]

But Armey's remarks went by wholly unnoticed. No newspaper I can recall has run a news item, nor have I read a single editorial condemning the Congressman's criminal remarks.

I can bet everything I own that if President Bush had publicly rebuked Armey in a speech, the media would not have glossed over the remarks.

Or take what America's top law enforcement official, Attorney General John Ashcroft, said about the religion of Islam back in Nov. 9, 2001, as quoted by conservative columnist Cal Thomas: "Islam is a religion in which God requires you to send your son to die for Him. Christianity is a faith in which God sends His son to die for you."[68]

In spite of thousands of protest letters and phone calls, in spite of calls from dozens of Arab-and Muslim-American and other civil liberties organizations, to John Ashcroft, the White House, and the media, to this day, the Attorney General has yet to take his words back, let alone apologize for his remarks. Worse, the remarks were simply ignored by the US media. It was not worth to build a story over, let alone issue an editorial, harsh or otherwise.

Why? Again, because the President didn't say, "go".

Then there are those outrages that have been perpetrated by the White House itself: the appointment of convicted liars John Poindexter and Elliot Abrams to key posts.

"Admiral Poindexter is somebody who this administration thinks is an outstanding American," Ari Fleischer said on February 25 of this year, after the appointment of Poindexter as head of DARPA. Then he went on to say, "[he is] an outstanding citizen who has done a very good job in what he has done for our country, serving in the military."[69]

This is the same John Poindexter who was convicted of conspiracy, lying to Congress, defrauding the government, and destroying evidence in the Iran Contra scandal. But instead of a hue of outrage, the media has remained relatively silent. As a result, Poindexter has now been elevated to the head the frighteningly named "Information Awareness Office". A convicted liar is now in charge of ferreting out the truth!

The same goes for Elliot Abrams, who in 1987 pleaded guilty to the charge that he withheld information from Congress on the Reagan administration's efforts to assist antigovernment guerrillas in Nicaragua." Back in July 2001, Abrams was appointed to the National Security Council staff as a senior director for democracy, human rights and international operations! Two weeks ago, he was appointed by President Bush to one of the most sensitive portfolios today, director of Middle Eastern affairs at the White House. No outcry was forthcoming in July 2001, and of course none two weeks ago.

Then there was the appointment of master of secrecy and duplicity Henry Kissinger to one of the most sensitive fact-finding missions in America's modern history; and of people well known for their contempt for the law and Congress, such as John D. Negroponte, who was ambassador to Honduras during the time that the contras were being given aid through that country in defiance of a law barring such aid (now ambassador to the United Nations), and Otto J. Reich, who was charged with running a covert domestic propaganda campaign against the Nicaragua government (now special envoy for western hemisphere affairs at the State Department).

Not one of these outrageous appointments has ruffled the media's feathers, let alone elicited their ire and indignation. Certainly not to the extent that Lott's remarks have.

The "war on terror" has taken a much heavier toll on our liberties than we might imagine if the media's sense of outrage needs to be prodded into life by a green light from The White House.

—December 17, 2002

Media failings in Middle East coverage

If we were living in a country where the mainstream press had the collective character and professional jealousy to make its own independent judgment about
news priorities, rather than by default safely defer to the daily briefings given by
the State Department, the White House, and the Department of Defense, the
following January 15, 2003, UPI story would have grabbed the headlines, or at
least made the front pages: "Israel is embarking upon a more aggressive approach
to the war on terror that will include staging targeted killings in the United States
and other friendly countries." As things stand, however, the story that Israel is
planning to carry out assassinations right here, on US soil, has simply been
treated as anything but that—as a non-story.[70]

Also a story not worthy of the media's attention is the following tid-bit from the
Washington Post: "[Israel's] state attorney, Talia Sasson, had argued that [Arab
Knesset Member Azmi] Bishara and his political party, Balad, should be banned
because they supported making Israel a state for all its citizens, which she said
would contradict Israel's founding principle as a Jewish state."[71] Is this the same
Jewish state touted as the only democracy in the Middle East, as the only haven
for the rule of law in a sea of anachronistic monarchies and thuggish regimes.
And yet, not a word of indignation from otherwise moralizing editorialists about
an official statement from the Israeli government that openly declares that Israel
is by definition not egalitarian, and that anyone who would propose that it
should be must be banned from participating in political life there.

We are now two years and four months into the Intifada. During this time,
Amnesty International, Human Rights Watch, B'tselem, and the United Nations
Human Rights Commission, to name just the most visible human rights groups,
have all reported in great detail, with striking consistency, and first hand, about
human rights violations suffered by Palestinians at the hands of the Israeli army.
And yet, the Associated Press, for instance, is still describing such human rights

129

violations as if they were mere "allegations" rather than established fact, or at least solidly reported findings. And so, we continue to read passages such as the following from a January 9, 2003, AP dispatch: "Media reports also claimed the [Israeli] government was furious at Britain's decision to block exports of critical spare parts for Israel's Phantom fighter planes because of alleged human rights abuses by Israeli troops in the West Bank and Gaza Strip."[72]

Could it be that the AP reporter for that story is simply not familiar with the findings of human rights groups? A very possible explanation, indeed, since some of their latest revelations have simply been ignored by the US mainstream media. For instance, little play has been given to a recent report from the Israeli human rights group B'tselem that accused the Israeli army of engaging in the practice of using Palestinian civilians as human shields, in direct violation of the Geneva Conventions as well as of rulings from the Israeli courts. In that report, "B'tselem exposes a list of incidents in which the IDF violated a High Court of Justice injunction by using Palestinians as human shields (as part of the "neighbor procedure").[73]

Little play has also been given to Amnesty International's September 3, 2002, statement on the Israeli High Court of Justice's ruling "allowing the forcible transfer of two Palestinians from their home town of Nablus to the Gaza Strip on the grounds that they allegedly assisted their brother to commit attacks against Israelis." Amnesty went on to say that "Today's ruling effectively allows for a grave violation of one of the most basic principles of international human rights law—notably the right of any accused to a fair trial and to challenge any evidence used against them."[74]

Such gross lapses in reporting could also explain why another AP reporter wrote the following on January 5, 2003, the day two suicide bombers detonated in Tel Aviv: "The bombings also ended a period of relative calm. Previously the last bombing inside Israel was Nov. 21, when 11 bus passengers were killed in Jerusalem."[75] Perhaps the reporter who wrote that story was not aware that during this "period of relative calm", B'tselem released a report which revealed that over 80% of Palestinians killed for "curfew violations" were children, many of them shot in the head, and that 70% of those killed in the month of December were children, women, and elderly.[76] If the AP reporter in question reads his news from the US mainstream media, indeed he would not know!

And if a reporter on the ground is so uninformed, what are the chances that we, more than two continents away, can even begin to grasp the magnitude of what is really happening there?

—January 27, 2003 (The Jordan Times)

Living in a world of myths

For those who are interested in studying how myths are born, how they are nurtured, how they take hold and mature to the point that they become unchallenged reality—at least until they are no longer useful and a young historian writes an astonishing breakthrough study that overturns those myths—the Israeli-Palestinian conflict offers us a unique object lesson that we should all heed if we are interested in building a future with a solid base of truth.

Contrary to the myth of Ehud Barak's generous offers and political courage in Camp David, 2000, the fact of the matter is that at the height of his "generosity", Ehud Barak insisted on keeping 80% of the settlers within Palestinian land. And he did this in spite of the fact that 69% of Israelis in general favor the evacuation of most or all settlements, while two-thirds of settlers have said time and again that they are willing to evacuate the Occupied Territories and would readily accept financial compensation and be resettled inside Israel. We often hear of Yasir Arafat's political cowardice. Why didn't Barak seize the moment and capitalize on the popular consensus that the settlers should come back home?[77]

Contrary to the prevailing myth that Palestinian text books are anti-Semitic and teach Palestinians to hate Israel, the fact of the matter, as reported by Professor Nathan Brown of George Washington University in a study published in November 2001, "The Palestinian curriculum is not a war curriculum; while highly nationalistic, it does not incite hatred, violence, and anti-Semitism. It cannot be described as a 'peace curriculum' either, but the charges against it are often wildly exaggerated or inaccurate."[78]

Contrary to the myth that the gap between the Palestinians and the Israelis was unbridgeable after Camp David, the fact of the matter is that had the Israelis continued talking with the Palestinians rather than declare the talks a dead end, a final settlement would probably have been reached by now, sparing the life of innocent Israelis and Palestinians. Proof of this is the fact that after the end of the Taba talks in January, 2001, Ehud Barak signed on the following joint statement with the Palestinians: "The two sides declare that they have never been closer to reaching an agreement and it is thus our shared belief that the remaining gaps could be bridged with the resumption of negotiations following the Israeli elections."[79]

Contrary to the myth that Ariel Sharon does accept the need for a Palestinian state, the fact of the matter is that a core principle of the Likud party's platform—the party he has headed for years—is its commitment that there shall be "No Palestinian state west of the Jordan river".[80] [4] Ariel Sharon has never moved to remove that clause from the platform. Another set of inconvenient facts that don't sit well with the myth of the wise and tough "man of peace" is the basic fact that Ariel Sharon has opposed every single peace treaty with the Arabs: As a member of Begin's cabinet, he voted against a peace treaty with Egypt; In 1985 he voted against the withdrawal of Israeli troops to the so-called security zone in Southern Lebanon; In 1991 he opposed Israel's participation in the Madrid peace conference; In 1993 he voted No in the Knesset on the Oslo agreement, and in the following year he abstained in the Knesset on a vote over a peace treaty with Jordan.; he voted against the Hebron agreement in 1997 and objected to the way in which the withdrawal from southern Lebanon was conducted."[81]

Contrary to the myth that the Palestinian Authority deliberately started the Intifada, the fact is that according to the Mitchell report, "[there is no basis] on which to conclude that there was a deliberate plan by the PA to initiate a campaign of violence at the first opportunity; or to conclude that there was a deliberate plan by the GOI [Government of Israel] to respond with lethal force."[82]

And contrary to the myth that the Arabs are hell-bent on destroying Israel, here is what the Arabs proposed when they gathered in Beirut on March 28, 2002—even while Ariel Sharon was launching his disastrous assault on Palestinians in the West Bank: "The Arab countries affirm the following: a. Consider the Arab-Israeli conflict ended, and enter into a peace agreement with Israel, and provide security for all the states of the region. b. Establish normal relations with Israel in the context of this comprehensive peace."

The question then is: why do these myths not only persist and but thrive and prosper in the landscape of American discourse about the Mideast conflict? In a country where freedom of speech was established precisely to ensure that lies can never take a foothold, why do so many falsehoods survive?

Perhaps that question too needs a future young historian who can answer it in era where those lies and falsehoods are no longer useful.

—January 29, 2003

Tune off and drop out, or tune in and speak out

I made it out right in time. I left Algiers, heading for Blacksburg, Virginia, via Paris then Washington, on January 15, 1991. On our way to the airport, my father asked me if I thought Bush was going to attack. "Yes, he is," I answered without hesitation. My answer seemed to catch him off guard. "Really?" he asked, impressed by the certainty of my response. "The Americans don't mobilize like that and just pull back," I explained, "besides, Congress has given him permission." He nodded, but I could see that he didn't really believe me. He still thought that it was a big bluff and that "in the end", the UN would work something out.

The next day, of course, the Allies started their attack, and I watched, like everyone else, the skies of Baghdad "light up", as CNN's Bernard Shaw and Peter Arnet put it from their room in the Al-Rashid hotel.

I watched the start of the attacks from the student lounge. Live. Everyone around me was stunned, watching in perfect silence. No comments, just young people staring at the large TV screen. As it happened, a reporter from the Roanoke Times was present among us. And so, she kicked into high gear and started interviewing students on the spot. Then, spotting my swarthy, Middle-Eastern face, she rushed towards me, cutting short the interview she was doing with an "average American", and asked me if I would be interviewed.

"Yes, of course," I said breathlessly.

"What do you think about what is happening?" she asked.

"I think this is a disaster," I answered, as she scribbled away. I was angry. I was shocked. Rationally, I knew that the Americans would attack, but now that they had, I was stunned.

"Bombing will not solve anything," I added, my anger rising. "This will only make matters worse. I don't understand why they are attacking, this won't solve anything."

The journalist scribbled away, nodding, then asked, almost mechanically: "What would you have preferred as a course of action to get him out of Kuwait?"

"Negotiations," I answered, "not war. War only makes things worse...."

Back in my apartment, that night I slept with the TV on all night, the war my flickering background. I drifted in and out of sleep, but I never lost sense of the reality of what had happened that night. The nightmare was on. It was real, and my heart was heavy.

I called the family the next morning. "You made it out on time, you rascal," my younger brother laughed soberly. His plan was to head back to work in England the following week, but now all bets were off. My mother was in near hysterics, but thankful that I had managed to leave "just in time". And my father almost congratulated me on the accurate prediction. "I am surprised," he said, "but we should have seen it coming."

The next few weeks until the formal surrender were sheer torture. The non-stop mindless propaganda from CNN and the rest of the news is intolerable. I feel insulted and abused. The reporters are basing all of their stories on the press-briefings given in large army tents. Actually, there are no stories, but "recaps" and "summaries". And no one is complaining, it seems. I am made to watch videos of "smart bombs" as generals and colonels patiently explain exactly in what way those grainy images illustrated US military prowess.

Valentine's day: reports from Iraq that at least 500 civilians have been killed by Stealth fighters dropping bombs on fortified underground facilities in Baghdad are dismissed by the Pentagon, and the US media, as crass propaganda.

I think it was about that time that I just tuned out and started altogether avoiding television and newspapers. The horrible spectacle of watching a whole nation embrace war was fraying my health. I had to drop out.

Twelve years later, things have changed quite a bit—but then again, 'plus ca change, plus c'est la meme chose'. American human shields are on the ground, in Iraq, and millions of Americans have taken to the streets the past few weeks and months, protesting and resisting the war-mongers. But still, anyone not toeing the line is dismissed, ignored, even jeered as a traitor.

This morning, watching C-SPAN, I hear Bill Kristol explain that it may have been OK for Americans to protest the war this past summer, but now that we have 150,000 troops in the region, it would "unconscionable" to expect the US to simply do nothing. The damage to America's reputation, he said, would be "incalculable". The quest to win arguments by pure military force, literally, it seems has begun in earnest.

And so I am tempted. I am tempted to tune off, drop out, for the sake of my mental well-being.

Or should should I instead tune in and I speak out this time?

—February 14, 2003

Missing the story

An example of how the Associated Press's shabby journalism contaminates coverage of the Palestinian-Israeli conflict in US media

No other story has illustrated the timidity of the US-based Associated Press about reporting negatively on Israel as has their reluctance to cover adequately the war crimes lawsuits that were brought against Ariel Sharon back in June 2001. AP's coverage of the February 12, 2003, ruling by the Belgian courts is a startlingly revealing example.

For the Israeli press, the story from Belgium was straightforward: once he leaves office, Ariel Sharon can be tried for war crimes and genocide. The Jerusalem Post, an Israeli newspaper that backs the Likud and right-winger factions, opened its story with the following: "Belgium could investigate war crimes charges against Prime Minister Ariel in connection with a series of massacres perpetrated by Israeli-backed Christian militiamen at the Sabra and Shatilla Palestinian refugee camps near Beirut, Lebanon, in 1982, but only after he is no longer prime minister, and thus stripped of diplomatic immunity, Belgium's Supreme Court of Appeals ruled on Wednesday." The more progressive Ha'aretz on its part started the story with: "Belgium's supreme appeals court ruled on Wednesday that a genocide lawsuit against Ariel Sharon could go ahead once he no longer enjoyed immunity as prime minister of Israel, the plaintiffs' lawyer said." The Jerusalem Post headlined it, "Belgian court rules Sharon could be charged with war crimes after ends term", while Haarztez headlined it, "Belgian court says Sharon can be probed after leaving office." (See below for full texts.)

But the US-based Associated Press, under the byline of CONSTANT BRAND, told an altogether different story—one that is grossly misleading and almost contradicts the one running in the Israeli press. When originally published, the story was headlined, "Belgian Court Bars Sharon War-Crimes Case", and opened with: "The Belgian Supreme Court threw out an appeal by a group of Palestinians on Wednesday to try Israeli Prime Minister Ariel Sharon for war crimes over a 1982 massacre in Lebanese refugee camps." Then in paragraph 8 we read, "The Supreme Court ruled Wednesday, however, that investigations could proceed against former Israeli army commander Amos Yaron, who was the only other one named in the original complaint filed with Belgian prosecutors two years ago."

Nowhere in the AP story, as originally published on February 12, 2003, were we told the crux of the ruling: that Ariel Sharon can be tried for war crimes once he leaves office. In other words, the real news was simply skipped! (The AP later corrected the story, and added to the first opening paragraph the following: "but didn't rule out trying the Israeli prime minister after he leaves office." See end of this document for the original AP story.)

This gross distortion of the real news about the February 12, 2003 ruling was replicated on February 13, across all the major newspapers that rely on AP for their foreign coverage. The result was for almost all US papers and other media outlets that ran the AP story, the headlines were along the lines of, "Belgian court rejects Sharon trial" (Chicago Tribune), "Belgian court won't try Sharon" (The Los Angeles Times), "Court rejects case against Sharon" (The Arizona Republic), "Belgium's Top Court Nixes Palestinian Appeal to Try Sharon for War Crimes" (FoxNews.com), "Belgian Court Bars Sharon War-Crimes Case" (The Seattle Post Intelligencer), to name just a few. Only a small minority even bothered to modify their headline to capture the important fact (the real story, as far as the rest of the world press was concerned) that the ruling was temporary, as in, "Belgian court: No war-crimes trial for Sharon, for now" (The Philadelphia Inquirer) and "Belgium rejects Sharon war-crimes trial—for now" (The Toronto Globe and Mail).

By sharp contrast, papers that did not rely on AP, such as the New York Times or the Washington Post, or those who used Reuters rather than AP, covered the story correctly. The headline from the New York Times was, "Sharon Faces Belgian Trial After Term Ends"; the Washington Post, "Court Approves Suit Against Sharon"; and from CNN.com, which based its story on a Reuters dispatch, "Belgium: Sharon war crimes suit can go ahead".

But given that the Associated Press boasts over 1,700 newspaper clients in the US alone, the sad fact is that for most Americans, the Belgium ruling was favorable to Sharon, and once again, the Palestinians were the sorry losers.

The real loser is the American public.

—February 15, 2003[83]

Enough French bashing!

In an exchange with FoxNews's Tony Snow this past Sunday, Senator John McCain delivered probably the most blunt denigration of France and the French people publicly articulated by a respected American politician to date in the current crisis over Iraq. To Mr. Snow's question as to whether or not the French and the Germans would eventually come around and support the United States, John McCain answered with the following below-the-belt non-sequitur: "The French remind a little bit of an aging actress of the 1940s who is still trying to dine out on her looks but doesn't have the face for it. For any nation to be great, they have to have a great purpose."[84]

Implied in these two feisty, vintage McCain, sentences is the notion that France is an "aging power" ("old Europe", as Rumsfeld put it), or even that it is no longer "a power", and that it is "without purpose". Bundled in that, of course, is the unassailable assertion that that the United States is "a great power", a "great nation", and that it has "a purpose".

If "greatness" is to be measured by who has the greatest arsenal for war and destruction, then there is no doubt that the Senator is right, and that United States, which spends more on defense than the next fifteen nations combined[85], is the most powerful nation on earth, and that France is not.

And if "purpose" is to be equated with a determination to remain the only superpower on earth, as openly articulated in president Bush's September 17, 2002, "National Security Strategy of the United States of America", and if it means unilaterally determining who represents a threat and who does not, who is a foe and who is not, and not hesitating to act alone if the rest of the world does not fall into step, then certainly the United States has purpose, and France does not.

But for those who don't equate "greatness" with the power to destroy and "purpose" with the obsession to rule unchallenged, the United States is not the greatest nation on earth, nor is the one with the right purpose.

For those who prefer to examine instead the major indices that measure the well being of the citizens that make up a country—the only meaningful measure of how a country is really doing—there is a different conclusion about where the United States and France stand in the spectrum of "greatness" and "purpose".

For instance, infant mortality in France is 4.4 (per 1,000 live births), while the United States stands at 6.7[86]; life expectancy in France is 78.8 years, while that in the US is 77.1 years[87]; only 5.6% of French children live in poverty, while a whopping 20.3% of American children live below the poverty line[88]; France spends 5.90% of its GNP on education, while the United States spends 5.30% (no surprise that the French have us beat in mathematics, reading, and science literacy)[89]. This, in spite of the fact that France's GDP per capita is at $25,400, while that of the United State is more than $10,00 greater than that at $36,300[90].

America, the most virtuous, the land of moral probity? Let's see how those sexually loose, philandering French stand up against the God-fearing Americans. The teen pregnancy rate (per 1,000 women aged 15-19) is 20.2 in France and 83.6 in the United States; the adolescent birth rate is 10.0 in France and 54.4 in the United States; and the abortion rate is 10.2 in France and 29.2 in the United States[91]. As for who has the more solid marriages: the divorce rate in France stands at 38.3 (per 1000 marriages), while that in the United States is at 54.8.[92]

The homicide rate in France is 1.7 (per 100,000), while that in the US is 8.2; the incarceration rate in France is 85 (per 100,000), while that in the US is 686 (by far the highest per-capita in the world)[93]. The average waste generated by the French per person per year is 304 kg, while that generated by the Americans is more than double that, at 864 kg[94]. On average, the French consume 4.34 oil equivalent tons of energy per year per person, while the Americans consume almost twice that, at 8.7 tons per person[95]; the French emit 1.81 tons of carbon dioxide per person per year, while the Americans emit four times that much, at 5.53[96]; and while the French are responsible for 1.7% of world pollution, the Americans are responsible for 25.2%.[97]

America, the most giving, the most generous? Tell that to the hungry of the world. While France spends 0.23% of its GNP on Foreign Development Assistance, the United States spends a miserable, miserly 0.11%—dead last among giving nations.[98]

America, the home of the First Amendment and freedom of speech, and the cradle of democracy and its ever-vigilant protector? Well, according the recently released Freedom of Press Index, the United States ranks 14th in the world in freedom of press, three places behind France[99]; as for beating the French in the democracy game, the fact is that in the French 2002 presidential elections, 79.71% of eligible French voters did register, while only 67.39% of American eligible voters registered (or were allowed to register) in the 2000 elections.[100]

I say enough self-serving French-bashing. Enough of this mindless arrogance from a nation full of itself, a nation so consumed by the illusion of its superiority that it expects all to give way to its will, no matter what. Let's first fulfill our obligation to our children, our families, our society, and to the planet on which we live, before we start casting stones.

—February 22, 2003

Endnotes

1. See: **http://www.globalexchange.org/campaigns/cuba/foodAndMeds/ healthImpact.html**

2. See my Ph.D. thesis, "Man, Society, and Knowledge, in the Islamist discourse of Sayyid Qutb," 1998, **http://scholar.lib.vt.edu/theses/ available/etd-3398-184043/unrestricted/Final.pdf**

3. Gila Svirsky, "Spreading the secret," IsraelInsider, July 15, 2002. See: **http://www.pmwatch.org/pmw/manager/features/ display_message.asp?mid=561**

4. "A Gaza Diary", Chris Hedges, Harper's Magazine, October, 2001—see: **http://www.pmwatch.org/pmw/features/gazadiary.html**

5. "Selective use of the terms 'terrorism' and 'retaliation' in news coverage of the Palestinian-Israeli conflict: September 2000, May, 2002", Palestine Media Watch, Washington DC, 2002—See: **http://www.pmwatch.org/pmw/boycottthepost/retaliation.pdf**

6. "Detailed analysis of news coverage of the Palestinian-Israeli conflict by the Philadelphia Inquirer: January 2001—March 2001", Palestine Media Watch, Philadelphia, PA, 2001—See: http://www.pmwatch.org/pmw/reports/042401report.html

7. "Selective use of the terms 'terrorism' and 'retaliation' in news coverage of the Palestinian-Israeli conflict: September 2000, May, 2002", Palestine Media Watcha, Washington DC, 2002—See: **http:// www.pmwatch.org/pmw/boycottthepost/retaliation.pdf**

8. Ari Shavit, "End of a journey," Ha'aretz, July 11, 2002. See: **http://www.pmwatch.org/pmw/manager/features/ display_message.asp?mid=560**

9. "Detailed analysis of news coverage of the Palestinian-Israeli conflict by the Philadelphia Inquirer: May 2001", Palestine Media Watch, Philadelphia, PA, 2001—See: **http://www.pmwatch.org/pmw/reports/042401report.html**

10. "A Gaza Diary", Chris Hedges, Harper's Magazine, October, 2001—see: **http://www.pmwatch.org/pmw/features/gazadiary.html**

11. "Excerpts: NPR Interview of Chris Hedges," National Public Radio, October 2001—See: http://64.226.129.19/pmw/manager/features/display_message.asp?mid=487

12. "Dear soldier, please kill a lot of Arabs," Yedioth Ahronoth, May 7, 2002—Original Hebrew: **http://www.ynet.co.il/NonReg/Ext/App/Billing/Registration/ CdaBillReg_LoginScreen/1,10075,00.html**. For a commentary on article, see http://www.ynet.co.il/home/0,7340,L-1049-1879848,00.html

13. Ultra-Orthodox Shas Party spiritual leader Rabbi Ovadia Yosef, in a sermon discussing Passover and God's wrath at Israel's enemies, 8 April 2001. BBC, Aril 10, 2001—http://news.bbc.co.uk/hi/english/world/middle_east/newsid_1270000/1270038.stm

14. "A Gaza Diary", Chris Hedges, Harper's Magazine, October, 2001—see: http://www.pmwatch.org/pmw/features/gazadiary.html; "Excerpts: NPR Interview of Chris Hedges," National Public Radio, October 2001—See: http://64.226.129.19/pmw/manager/features/display_message.asp?mid=487

15. Dick Armey, MSNBC Hardball, May 1, 2002. http://www.pmwatch.org/pmw/indexarmey.asp

16. "New responses to Palestinian terrorism", Alan Dershowitz, Jerusalem Post, March 11, 2002. http://cgis.jpost.com/cgi-bin/General/printarticle.cgi?article=/Editions/2002/03\ /11/Opinion/Opinion.44919.html

17. "Hard-line Israeli supporters boo Wolfowitz", Washington Times, April 15, 2002—http://www.washtimes.com/upi-breaking/15042002-045834-6177r.htm

18. "John Ashcroft and Islam", Christopher G. Adamo, March 3, 2002—http://www.conservativetruth.org/archives/christopheradamo/03-03-02.shtml

19. "Camp David and After: An Exchange (1. An Interview with Ehud Barak)", June 13,

The New York Review of Books—http://www.nybooks.com/articles/15501

20. "Human Rights Watch: Israeli army committed war crimes against the Palestinians"—Arabic News, May 4, 2002—
http://www.arabicnews.com/ansub/Daily/Day/020504/2002050411.html

21. "Likud rejects Palestine statehood", Soraya Sarhaddi Nelson and Alfonso Chardy, Knight Ridder News Service—http://www.philly.com/mld/inquirer/3252945.htm

22. "Israeli settlements in the Occupied Territories: A Guide. A Special Report of the Foundation for Middle East Peace", Foundation for Middle East Peace, March 2002—http://www.fmep.org/reports/2002/sr0203.html#5

23. UN Resolution 242—http://www.pmwatch.org/pmw/snakebite/UN.html#_Toc522031722

24. UN Resolution 465—http://www.pmwatch.org/pmw/snakebite/UN.html#_Toc522031724

25. "America Can Persuade Israel to Make a Just Peace", April 21, 2002—The New York Times
http://www.andrew.cmu.edu/user/amandab/carter.html

26. "Sharm El-Sheikh Fact-Finding Committee Final Report," (The Mitchell Report)—May 23, 2001—
http://usinfo.state.gov/regional/nea/mitchell.htm

27. "Democracy, History, and the contest over the Palestinian curriculum," Nathan Brown, The George Washington University—
http://www.nad-plo.org/textbooks/nathan_textbook.pdf

28. "NPR Interview with Chris Hedges," October 30, 2001: http://64.226.129.19/pmw/manager/features/display_message.asp?mid=487

29. Joint Statement, signed by Ehud Barak's negotiating team, Taba, Egypt, January 27, 2001—http://www.mfa.gov.il/mfa/go.asp?MFAH0j7o0

30. "New report: land grab"—B'tselem report—May 13, 2002—http://www.btselem.org/English/Press_Releases/2002/020513.asp

31. "Arab Peace Initiative: full text", March 28, 2002—
http://www.guardian.co.uk/Print/0,3858,4383912,00.html

32. "Jenin War Crimes Investigation Needed," Human Rights Watch, may 3, 2002—**http://hrw.org/press/2002/05/jenin0503.htm**

33. See: http://www.pollingreport.com/israel.htm

34. Is the pro-Israel media lobby losing its grip?", Eric Boehlert, Salon.com, 4/17/2002.   See: http://www.pmwatch.org/pmw/manager/features/ display_message.asp?mid=542

35. Ibid.

36. Ibid.

37. "Poll shows Americans' support for Israel in decline", June 13, 2002—The Jerusalem Post,
http://www.pmwatch.org/pmw/manager/features/
display_message.asp?mid=543. In reaction to these findings, Ira Forman, director of the National Jewish Democratic Committee, said: "The poll signifies we have a lot of work, both as Republicans and as Democrats, with the American public…. Much too large a percentage of the American population thinks our policy is skewed toward Israel. That's very wrong."

38. Aaron Brown, "Israeli Warplanes Strike Target in Gaza Strip; Another Big Down Day on Wall Street; What Is Best Way to Rebuild Ground Zero?" NewsNight transcript, July 22, 2002—See: **http://www.cnn.com/TRANSCRIPTS/0207/22/asb.00.html**

39. Aaron Brown, "White House Criticizes Israeli Attack in Gaza; Dow Staggers to Close; 'Turner Diaries' Author Dies", NewsNight Transcript, July 23,   2002—See: **http://www.cnn.com/TRANSCRIPTS/0207/23/ asb.00.html**

40. Edward S. Herman, "'Tragic errors' as an integral component of policy", Z Magazine, September 2002.

41. Robert Fisk, "Pity the nation: Lebanon at war", Oxford University Press, 1990, 1992, 2001.

42. Chris Hedges, "A Gaza Diart," Harper's Magazine, October, 2001—See: **http://www.harpers.org/online/gaza_diary/?pg=1**

43. Chris Hedges, Interview on NPR's Fresh Air, October 30, 2001—See: **http://www.pmwatch.org/pmw/cast/hedges.asp**

44. Rania Awwad, Ahmed Bouzid, Rani El-Hajjar, Mazin Qumsiyeh, "Israel does target civilians: documented evidence," Palestine Media Watch, September, 2002
    —See: **http://www.pmwatch.org/pmw/essays/civilians.html**

45. Private communication by email, June 4, 2002.

46. Ibid.

47. Nolan Finley, "Israel's children are the target of Middle East terror campaign," The Detroit News, March 17, 2002—See:
    http://www.detnews.com/2002/editorial/0203/17/a15-442135.htm
    and **http://www.pmwatch.org/pmw/cast/detnews.asp**

48. "Blatant example of double standards and uncritical adoption by US press of the Israeli spin," Palestine Media Watch, June 27, 2002—See: **http://www.pmwatch.org/pmw/reports/tally/**

49. "How US papers covered the July 22, 2002, Gaza bombing," Palestine Media Watch, Sept. 7, 2002—see:
    http://www.pmwatch.org/pmw/reports/tally/072302.html

50. "Report on the Philadelphia Inquirer's front-page pictures on the Palestinian-Israeli conflict," Palestine Media Watch, August 2, 2002—See: **http://www.pmwatch.org/pmw/reports/pi/frontpage/frontpage.html**

51. "Report of the Secretary-General prepared pursuant to General Assembly resolution ES-10/10 (Report on Jenin)", United Nations, August 1, 2002—See: **http://www.un.org/peace/jenin/index.html**

52. Email communication forwarded by a member of Palestine Media Watch who complained directly to Mr. Lundy.

53. "In Washington Post, Palestinians attack, Israel retaliates," Palestine Media Watch, May 1, 2002—See:
    http://www.pmwatch.org/pmw/cast/retaliationwp.asp

54. "'Vigilantes' vs. 'Terrorists': Enough of double standards from the Washington Post", Palestine Media Watch, March 13, 2002—See:
    http://www.pmwatch.org/pmw/cast/vigilante.asp

55. Dan Fisher, "Pejorative or descriptive? Blanket rules on using 'terrorist' don't cover every case", MSNBC, March 20, 2002—See:
    http://www.pmwatch.org/pmw/cast/msnbcandterror.asp

56. "Pressure points," NewsHour, PBS, July 3, 2002—See: **http:// www.pbs.org/newshour/bb/media/july-dec02/media_7-3.html**

57. "CNN still refuses to set up web memorial for innocent Palestinian victims", Palestine Media Watch, July 15, 2002—See: **http://www.pmwatch.org/pmw/cast/cnnbias5.asp.** It is worth pointing out that CNN finally

58. Ibid.

59. "Adding insult to injury: 'Palestinian fatalities' gallery another vivid illustration of double standard", Palestine Media Watch, September 5, 2002—See: **http://www.pmwatch.org/pmw/cast/cnnbias12.asp**

60. An abridged version of this essay appeared in Editor & Publisher (September 23, 2002).

61. http://www.childrensdefense.org/childwatch/column/2002_401.php

62. http://www.cia.gov/cia/publications/factbook/fields/2004.html

63. http://www.worldpolicy.org/projects/arms/reports/israel050602.html

64. http://www.cbsnews.com/stories/2002/12/04/politics/main531683.shtml

65. http://www.af.mil/news/Dec2002/121202250print.shtml

66. http://www.pmwatch.org/pmw/cast/armey.asp#TRANSCRIPT

67. **http://www.pmwatch.org/pmw/cast/armey2.asp**

68. **http://www.aaiusa.org/pr/release02-08-02.htm**

69. Press Briefing by Ari Fleischer, White House Press Secretary, February 25, 2002 **http://www.fas.org/sgp/news/2002/02/wh022502.html**

70. http://www.pmwatch.org/pmw/mediocrity/displayCall.asp?essayID=58

71. http://www.pmwatch.org/pmw/mediocrity/displayCall.asp?essayID=55

72. http://www.pmwatch.org/pmw/mediocrity/displayCall.asp?essayID=54

73. http://www.btselem.org/English/Publications/Full_Text/Human_Shield/index.asp

74. http://www.pmwatch.org/pmw/cast/aijeninreport.asp

75. http://www.pmwatch.org/pmw/mediocrity/displayCall.asp?essayID=45

76. **http://www.pmwatch.org/pmw/cast/80percent.asp**

77. "Study find most settlers willing to evacuate", Peace Now, July 24, 2002. See: http://www.pmwatch.org/pmw/manager/features/ display_message.asp?mid=562

78. "Democracy, history, and the contest over the Palestinian curriculum," November, 2001. See: http://www.nad-plo.org/textbooks/nathan_textbook.pdf. See also: http://www.pmwatch.org/pmw/cast/textbookcanard.asp

79. Joint Statement, signed by Ehud Barak's negotiating team, Taba, Egypt, January 27, 2001—Joint Statement, signed by Ehud Barak's negotiating team, Taba, Egypt, January 27, 200. See: http://www.nybooks.com/articles/15502

80. See Palestine Media Watch, "Enough whitewashing Israeli rejectionism," Palestine Media Watch, May 14, 2002. See http://www.pmwatch.org/ pmw/cast/rejectionism.asp

81. Alexander Cockburn, "The Crimes of Ariel Sharon", Counterpunch, February 7th 2001. http://www.counterpunch.org/sharon.html

82. "Sharm El-Sheikh Fact-Finding Committee Final Report," Sharm El-Sheikh Fact-Finding Committee, May 23, 2001. See: **http:// usinfo.state.gov/regional/nea/mitchell.htm**

83. The Full report on AP is at: **http://www.pmwatch.org/pmw/reports/ap/ ap021403.html**—For the complete database of PMWATCH reports, see: **http://www.pmwatch.org/pmw/reports/**

84. Fox News, February 16, 2003 http://www.evote.com/index.asp?Page=/ weekend_section/02162003/FOXReview.asp

85. Major U.S. Foreign Policy Challenges, Claremont College, The Hon. Lee H. Hamilton, November 12, 2002 **http://216.239.57.100/ search?q=cache:ihS1xOglLpUC:wwics.si.edu/docs/staff/ Hamilton_usfpchall.doc+%22spends+more+on+defense+than+the+n ext+fifteen+nations+combined%22&hl=en&ie=UTF-8**

86. U.S. Census Bureau, International Database, 2002—http:// www.infoplease.com/ipa/A0004393.html—http://www.skepticism.net/ articles/2002/000022.html

87. U.S. Census Bureau's International Data Base, 2000—http://geography.about.com/library/weekly/aa042000b.htm—http://geography.about.com/library/weekly/aa042000b.htm

88. Vlemincks and Smeeding (eds) Child Well-being, Child Poverty and Child Policy in Modern Nation—http://www.maxwell.syr.edu/news/releases/child_poverty_map.html

89. University of Pennsylvania/Graduate School of Education, International Literacy Explorer—http://www.literacyonline.org/explorer/countriesselect.html

90. The World Factbook, 2002—http://www.cia.gov/cia/publications/factbook/fields/2004.html

91. Susheela Singh and Jacqueline E. Darroch, "Adolescent Pregnancy and Childbearing: Levels and Trends in Developed Countries", Volume 32, No. 1, January/February 2000—http://www.agi-usa.org/pubs/journals/3201400.html

92. Gulnar Nugman, "World divorce rates", the Heritage Foundation, 2002—http://www.divorcereform.org/gul.html

93. Handgun Control, "America still leads industrialized world in handgun homicide, despite gains made since Brady law"—http://www.bradycampaign.org/press/release.asp?Record=111

94. Michael Wolff, Peter Rutten, Albert Bayers III, eds., and the World Rank Research Team, "Where We Stand", (New York: Bantam Books, 1992)—http://www.korpios.org/resurgent/L-pollutioncomparisons.htm

95. Handbook of Energy and Economic Statistics in Japan—http://www.eccj.or.jp/result/eng/13.html

96. "Carbon Dioxide Fact Sheet, 2001"—http://pages.ca.inter.net/~jhwalsh/wfsesr.html

97. "Carbon Dioxide Fact Sheet, 2001"—http://pages.ca.inter.net/~jhwalsh/wfsesr.html

98. "Net ODA flows in 2000, 2001", Organization for Economic Cooperation and Development—**http://www.globalissues.org/TradeRelated/Debt/USAid.asp**—http://www.globalissues.org/TradeRelated/Debt/USAid.asp

99. Reporters Without Borders, "Reporters Without Borders publishes the first worldwide press freedom index", October 2002—http://www.rsf.fr/article.php3?id_article=4116

100. International Institute for Democracy and Electoral Assistance—**http://www.idea.int/vt/index.cfm**

0-595-27215-0

www.ingramcontent.com/pod-product-compliance
Lightning Source LLC
Chambersburg PA
CBHW061253280526
45784CB00002B/750